Creating an intelligent content management to have intelligent customer relationship management in e-commerce websites

Abstract

Internet and information technology (IT) has influenced on human modern world so that he/she has no more solution except to use the Internet to meet his needs, do his/her daily affairs, follow up modern world issues, and make a relation with others. Human needs and meeting his/her needs were categories which established business world. The main focus of business ranging from barter, as the most basic practices of business, to pecuniary exchange, is customer and her/his needs. Businesses found more incomes and profits resulted by more sales.

Seller and buyer are present in physical relationships between humans and their interactions to perform business dealings, so the seller can make relation with customer to know his needs by using customer management sciences and psychologies necessary for understanding customer needs. The most important and difficult part of the sales is to identify customer needs and they are not well known, but to identify the customer itself. Customer identification in terms of tastes, personality and psychology are as important as understanding of his /her needs. When the seller knows his/her customers, even the kind of deal between them takes a special form. Identify the customer and his/her needs lead to satisfy his/her needs at best. It has a completely unconscious impact on increasing customer confidence. When the customer confidence increases, its effect on his/her loyalty can be felt. The ultimate goal of any business is customer loyalty.

The thesis tries to create intelligent and targeted management in websites content by intelligent agents. The aim of management is to create customer relationship management which establishes an intelligent relationship to identify the customer and to continue to keep and improve customer confidence by specific marketing techniques and to make loyalty in customer. As mentioned before, customer loyalty is the ultimate goal of any business. The thesis tries to create an intelligent business website so that it begins with bilateral interaction between the customer and the web. Web content will take an action to identify the customer by intelligent agents for customer relationship management science and continue its management to complete web customer process.

Contents

6-2 Future studies

Resources

List of Tables

Title

List of figures

Title

Chapter 1

Introduction

Internet and information technology (IT) has influenced on human modern world so that he/she has no more solution except to use the Internet to meet his needs, do his/her daily affairs, follow up modern world issues, and make a relation with others. Human needs and meeting his/her needs were categories which established business world. The main focus of business ranging from barter, as the most basic practices of business, to pecuniary exchange, is customer and her/his needs. Businesses found more incomes and profits resulted by more sales. Since many suppliers and producers are in business age and provide consumers with necessary materials in modern world, competition is natural for obtaining more income. But competition method and ability of customer and market attraction are very important. According to a Chinese proverb: "It is very easy to open a business but is an art to keep it [47]"

Seller and buyer are present in physical relationships between humans and their interactions to perform business dealings, so the seller can make relation with customer to know his needs by using customer management sciences and psychologies necessary for understanding customer needs. The most important and difficult part of the sales is to identify customer needs and they are not well known, but to identify the customer itself. [1]

Customer needs will be met by existing facilities when they are identified. There are some factors such as price, quality, goods and special conditions of products needed by customer after identifying his need. [1] .But sales are not the only important factor to keep a successful business. When a business can convert a potential customer to actual one, it should consider that customer retention to meet his/her needs can cause and stabilize a business income and profit. Then business competition to attract a customer as a primary step and to keep him/her in second step can be called as a key factor in reaching to successful business. [1]

So many new ideas have been discussed about e-business in recent years. These ideas have presented new approaches to create applicable value by new technology tools such as comprehensive application of Internet and it's technologies-based. E-business interest and trend were maximized in 1998 and 1999. It has recently been shown that many of the ideas have not been successful. Many economic businesses used e- business could not take advantage of their business ideas. Many companies relied on e-business future profits went bankrupt. One main reason for the failure of these ideas is to not create value for customers. In addition, many of these ideas have not been profitable enough for the firms. One of key problems in new e-business ideas is that they have primarily been adjusted unclearly and most of time they don't explain business exactly. Consequently, many initiative ideas of new business are somehow dispersive and incorrect and it makes idea performance and information system development a difference [1]. The necessary issue is to describe idea process more deeply. To better understand each idea, it is necessary to adjust them at best possible form and highest accuracy and details and to emphasize on dimensions applicable in terms of economic and technical perspectives. E-Commerce has entered many ideas, theories and techniques in business as a new business model but the point not to be forgotten is that business tools only has been changed and no more change has been made in business principals. Therefore, new model should be made in compliance with business principals to reach business objectives.

1-1 Statement of problem

Seller and buyer don't face physically to each other in e-commerce and e-business. So there is no sense of human interaction. With regard to create new conditions for virtual communication world, Businesses need new approaches to establish relationship with customer in e-commerce , so new issues about behavioral patterns for customer relationship and specific relationship psychologies will be discussed. Business competition in Internet virtual world won't be similar to the physical world anymore. [1] Competitors, businesses and customers are all in Internet. They are all along together with no distance being felt. Here the competition will have more meaning. Here there is no one who cries and leads customers into the stores. The web contents can attract customers. The slightest Internet neglect makes competitor to change the result to his benefit. [1] As already mentioned, two important issues are key success factors in business: 1. Customer attract and 2. Customer retention. Customer retention is associated with commitment and loyalty. [13]

Customer identification in terms of tastes, personality and psychology are as important as understanding of his /her needs. When the seller knows his/her customers, even the kind of deal between them takes a special form. Customer identification and his/her needs lead to satisfy his/her needs at best. It has a completely unconscious impact on increasing customer confidence. When the customer confidence increases, its effect on his/her loyalty can be felt. The ultimate goal of any business is customer loyalty.

The article tries to study issues related to content management and customer relationship management method by using semantic web, ontology, data mining, websites, and smart database in order that it creates a pattern for e-commerce websites and improves power of customer attraction and retention.

1-2 Importance of issue

Business success and its retention are very critical. As mentioned before, according to a Chinese proverb: "It is very easy to open a business but is an art to keep it [47]". A business is successful when it can always have customer or purchaser to buy its products. Customer attraction and convenience to buy for the first time are very important. This requires specific art and ability in Internet and Web, because everything is virtual with no mutual understanding. Following the above mentioned, to keep customer satisfaction from his/her purchase causes confidence and loyalty which are the main reasons why he/she comes back to purchase and next interactions.[13]

An e-commerce can be successful when it continues to keep virtual business and it is not realized unless it uses comprehensive and targeted content management according to organizational objectives to earn more money by using specific initiatives as compared to its competitors. In result, modern world technologies must be given to customers to implement mutual understanding and cognition somehow in virtual world such that no distance is felt between customer and seller (website). This is done only if businesses can identify their customers and manage them and their relationship to present targeted web content accordingly.

1-3 Research Questions

• How does e-business modeling process help to better understand and identify the business elements in the organization?

• How can basic factors of different customers be categorized to make a more comprehensive decision for interaction against different behaviors?

• Where is content management in business model software?

• How can intelligent content management in e-commerce websites provide our final goal with creating an intelligent relationship customer management?

• What are advantages of making customer relationship management smart for the organization?

1-4 Research objectives

We study theory of intelligent content generation model dynamically in such a way that various types of customer behaviors are designed and implemented differently and according to fully personal customers' needs. Intelligent customer relationship management in e-business will be resulted by implementing the research which is based on business ontology and provide the business with model view.

The theoretical bases and concepts used during the study will be presented in Chapter 2. Then previous studies will be reviewed in Chapter 3. In this chapter, we will bring you examples of works and theories done in previous years. We will discuss our proposed plan in chapter 4 and bring an example for elaborating the proposed plan in chapter 5. Finally, the conclusions of the discussions will be presented in Chapter 6.

Chapter 2
Theoretical bases

We define and interpret necessary concepts and principles used during the study in this chapter.

2-1 E-commerce

Business phenomenon which is now called "e-commerce" has an interesting history. It grew rapidly in mid 1990 to 2000. But it disappeared due to economic recession from 2000 to 2003. Not only the remaining companies of economic recession developed sales, but also obtained a lot of profits. We have been faced with annual growing e-commerce since then. [2]

2-1-1 E-commerce and E-business [1]

Many people knows the term e-commerce as Internet purchase while it includes all business activities such as deals, internal business agent process , design, sales and support used IT for transfer e-data. E-business is a more comprehensive term that refers to any activities conducted on the World Web Network (Internet).

E-commerce, e-banking, e-government, e-citizenship, e-tourism, etc. are all examples of e-business. E-commerce is divided into five general categories with regard to type of business:

1. Business to government (B2G)
2. Business to Business (B2B)
3. Business to Customer (B2C) (customer means people)
4. Customer to Customer (C2C)
5. Business Processes

Business processes include group of services provided by e-business and cause to facilitate business affairs, while three government, business and people groups use them such as financial transfer provided by e-banking. Among above groups, three ones are the most important and functional including 2, 3 and 5 groups which are shown as components of e-commerce in figure 2-1.

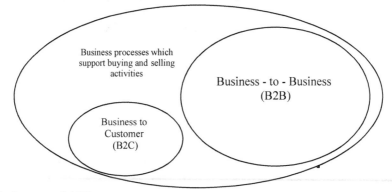

Business processes which support buying and selling activities

Business - to - Business (B2B)

Business to Customer (B2C)

2-1-2 Business model [1]

Business model is the method of relationship between set of processes combined with each other to create the benefit. It is expected that a good business model leads to rapid growth in sales and dominates the market. This theory, which is the simplest way of successful businesses modeling, is not effective factor or struggle for market retention in many businesses. When business analyzers were informed of the sudden dot-com fall in Recession periods, they suspected about performance and efficiency of business model so that Michael Porter said that not only business model are not important but also has no external existence.

It is obvious that Companies use Copyright rule or adapt themselves with other business models have no simple way to gain success. They must identify the elements involved with their business in order to identify business processes which are movable, replaceable or transferable with processes derived from Internet technology .Some companies and investors still use the theory of income model including specific set of business processes used for identifying customer, marketing customer and making availability sales for customer. The theory of income model is appropriate for classification of income-earning activities, communication and analysis.

2-1-3 Advantages of e-commerce [1]

Advantages of E-commerce can be as follows:

1. E-commerce increases sales and reduces cost.
2. E-commerce provides wider range of choices for buyers as compared to traditional business.
3. A 24 hour search has caused no time limitation for customers because some customers prefer to have full

information to make a good decision for the merchandise. Internet provides them with all needed information by only single click and they don't need to spend some days to gather necessary information.

4. The advantages of e-commerce have spread to the general welfare of community, such as e-banking.

5. Unlimited place is the other e-commerce advantage which has caused accessibility to any distance.

2-1-4 Disadvantages of e-commerce [1]

Most of the disadvantages of e-commerce is derived from innovation and rapid technology development. However, many of the disadvantages will be lost entirely by e-commerce growth, providing more opportunities and etc. However, some of them are as follows:

1. Some business processes may never be among the e-commerce. For example, perishable foods, or expensive goods and items like jewelry and antiques.

2. Reverse of Investment (ROI) parameter is estimated by most businesses before establishing any committee to purchase and use new technologies. Such estimation is very difficult in e-commerce because there is no simple way to compute profit and cost in the e-commerce world. Cost is very hard to calculate because of rapid changing of technology.

3. It is difficult to integrate existing database and necessary software design to change business from traditional to e-commerce.

4. Many businesses face to cultural and legal barriers. For example, many customers still distrust to send their credit card numbers over the Internet.

2-2 E-Commerce Web Sites

According to expertise estimation, e-commerce websites have disappointed over 75% customers such that they leave website without any purchase due to designing type. The best websites have even lost half of their customers due to problem in using the websites.[1]

An important part of a successful e-commerce performance is website which plays the role of potential customers interaction. Web sites are the only customers-businesses interface. The salesman techniques for shop selling and buying have no meaning in the Internet virtual world. There is shop no longer to attract customers by beautiful and absorbing decorations and draw them into the store. In Internet, website must plays both the role of shop beautiful decoration and skillful seller to establish relationship customer and finally to complete selling and buying process. Hence the design and produce e-commerce Web sites are very important.

Successful businesses know that every Web visitor is a potential customer. The most important concern is different strategies they must show in their business websites with regard to a variety of visitor characteristics, while all people don't visit a website for one purpose and it hardly happens that a person enters to a web suddenly. So Web designers have to design a site useful for everyone.

2-2-1 Basic knowledge and primary stages

The followings are very important separately before commercial Web sites are designed by web designers.

First step: familiarity with three basic types of commercial Web sites.

1. International websites

2. B2B websites

3. B2C websites

Step Two: Using answers to the following questions determines the kind of website.

1. What is the firm's business goal?

2. How will it have customers?

3. How the information will be provided by the website to visitors?

Step Three:

1. Determine the domain name

2. Determine the webpage content alongside with organizational objectives

3. Determine the web look and feel

4. Determine the navigation structure of website

5. Additional elements needed in e-commerce.

6. Identify services to Customers

7. Determine the method of buying process, shopping card and payment terms on the Web.

Step Four: Specify the website host and consider the following factors:

1. What services can be received from a web host?

2. Which services are compatible with our web organizational structure and services?

3. How to use the dedicated server against host service

4. Being aware of the Down-Time

5. Services provided by the host as after-sales services and how to provide them

2.2.2 Usability of the Web

Usability of website is defined by IEEE Association Standard dictionary as: simplicity in learning how to work with the Web site, preparation of input data and interpretation of the output content. Usability of website is so important that is known as the key for the following factors.

• The key to human-computer interactions (HCI)

• Main focus on web design

• The result by web technology evolution

Usability of website has considerable importance for e-commerce Web sites due to the followings. [1]

• Web site, the most basic customer-business interface.

• Web site, immediate satisfaction element of instant customer expectations.

• Usability of website is an experience that will have a direct impact on customer commitment to purchase.

• Usability of website is justifiable expect by the customer.

• Web world Competition is defined only by one click.

• Usability of website is defined as a time-consuming factor for data browser.

• Usability of website is one of critical success factors in web design projects.

• E-Commerce Web Sites = Free Shops

• The e-commerce websites= e-seller

• E-commerce Web sites = online catalogs in direct sales

2-2-3 Conversion rate

Conversion rate is percentage derived by number of web visitor's ratio who conducted specific action on web to total number of visitors.[3] The mentioned "specific action" can be defined in different ways, for example:

• Navigation on Web pages other than main page

• Purchase by the Web

• Register on the Web

• Register for receiving News

• And etc.

In business website, the more conversion rate increases, the more success achieve in customer attracts usability and finally web business performance. Or in other words, it can be said that the conversion rate of potential customers into actual customers is higher. Increasing this parameter depends on factors such as: [4]

• customer interest

• attractive website content

• Easy to perform processes on the Web

Customer interest maximizes when his/her need to be met at the right time. But attractive website content is as follows:

• User Interface

• Convenience

• Performance

• Effecting Advertising

Usability and e-commerce Web sites marketing can be called effective factors on the conversion rate. These factors can influence on the following in any obvious way:

1. Inappropriate audience (marketing)

2. Unclear marketing messages (Marketing)

3. Slow page load on users computer (usability)

4. Formation of an unengaging look and feel in users (usability)

5. Clumsy site navigation (usability)

6. Ineffective content presentation (usability)

7. Inadequate and improper selection (usability)

8. No-Access to real time help (usability)

9. Uncompetitive prices with market prices (marketing)

10. Ineffective tools to assist a good selection (usability)

The above factors and their effect on the conversion rate can be seen more accurately in Figure 2-2. [5]

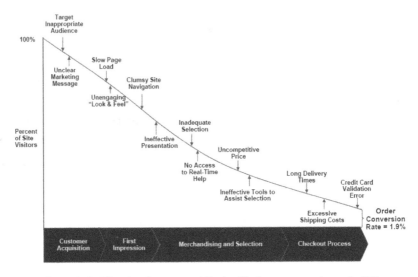

Figure 2-2: Effective factors and their effect on conversion rate [5]

As you can see in Figure 2-2, the left-right horizontal axis is route stages of customer on the website. Vertical axis is the percentage of website visitors. The graphic curve shows that the percentage of website visitors is high in the first stage. But the more customer delays on web or moves on horizontal axis (above figure), the more mentioned negative factors on curve decreases number of visitors.

2-2-4 Website creditability

One of the most important parameters in business is creditability. Traders and investors believe that creditability is the greatest capital a person or business can have to keep his/her business. In the business world, creditability is like a capital of a trader and there is no difference between them. How is business creditability evaluated in e-commerce? One of the parameters to assess it is to evaluate website creditability.

1. Real web feel by Customer
2. Easy of web use by Customer
3. Website expertise
4. Customer trustworthiness
5. Web Design
6. Commercial concepts implication.
7. Amateurism

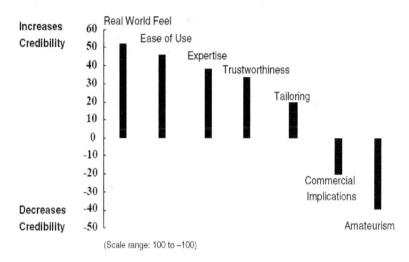

(Scale range: 100 to –100)

Figure 2-3: Effective factors and their effect on Website creditability [6]

2-2-5 Customer- oriented [1]

The Website design generally can be divided into two different ways.

1. Static

2. Dynamic

Today, the only method used and approved for designers and implementers of e-commerce websites is the dynamic method. In this way, Web content is generated dynamically as well. The advantage of this approach is independent website structure from information contained in the database. When data Changes in the database, the website structure makes no change but its content does. It can be found by the above mentioned that the customer plays an important role in e-commerce. A business customer will ensure the permanency of business. The E-commerce Web sites design, introduced as the only user interface between customer and business, is of high importance. The customer-oriented architecture of e-commerce Web sites design was idea in which designers only consider customer and its related factors to improve usability of website for customer and finally increase conversion rate. The following parameters can be mentioned as effective factors of customer-oriented architecture th:

• Customer needs

• Customer expectations

• Customer experience

• Customer convenience when using the Website

The most important achievement of customer-oriented architecture in e-commerce Web sites design is personalization which has not reached to the desired abstract limit yet. Because virtual interactions are free from perception and feel and cannot understand the customer's feeling. The whole personalization discussion is summarized in range of limited options which designers providing customers with services by their Web sites. For example, change the background color or select a specific pattern to look website. These are correct, but they don't transfer mutual understanding from the website to the customer.

2-3 Semantic Web 24 [7]

Semantic Web can be imagined as a global space by intelligent mechanic computation in which all books, libraries, knowledge, universities and knowledge bases are arranged as meaning-oriented and conceptual ability. Mr. Tim Burners Lee known as a father of web has explained the web future in such a way that it is not understand only by humans but can be understood and processed by machines, in spite of current web. The idea of semantic Web is originated by this point. Thee different definitions of the Semantic Web are presented as follows:

• Semantic Web is the project aiming at creates a global medium for exchange of information in such a way that it can be understood and processed for computer.
• Semantic Web is a network of global-scale information in a way that their processing is easily possible by machines.
• Semantic Web includes intelligent Web data that can be processed by machines.

Although close to achieving such a space needs new and holistic development in many courses such as engineering, mathematical, IQ, especially in linguistic, philosophy and much other knowledge, initial steps have been taken in this regards.

2-3-1 Semantic web components

Many standards and tools related to XML technology (Extensible Markup Language) can be also attributed to future Internet and the Semantic Web. Some technologies including XML schema, Resource Description Framework (RDF), RDF schema, and Web Ontology Language (OWL) can also mentioned. Various components of the Semantic Web have been shown in the Figure 2-4.

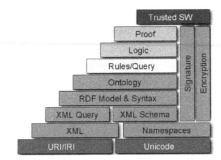

Figure 2-4: Components of the Semantic Web [7]

RDF is basic language used in the Semantic Web and has been based on XML. XML has also been based on Unicode and it supports different languages. The URI is used to define the concepts of the Semantic Web, for example, URL is a kind of URI that is used to determine the web resources. The main part of semantic Web is ontology which establishes the relationship between semantic Web document labels and the actual objects which describe their documents. On the top of the ontology exists rules that new knowledge can be deduced from existing knowledge. If a standard framework is created for existing rules, they can be proved and finally the obtained proves can be shared in different application. One of the goals of semantic Web is to ensure that it places in the highest layer. Thus, various standards are emerging and being used accordingly. Among these standards, FOAF (Friend of a Friend) can be called as a standard for social networking.

2-3-2 Resources description language

Hyper Text Markup Language (HTML) used in current web can not describe objects and their relationships on the web. So the other language has been created to use in the Semantic Web which is called *resources description language*. [7]

RDF: is a XML-based language to describe concepts and create documents in the Semantic Web. In fact, RDF documents contain information about the semantic web in a way that makes them understandable to machines. As shown in Figure 2-5, each phrase is expressed in three parts of subject, predicate and object in RDF. Predicate and its subject are the resource and object is also the resource or literal. There are also tools to display RDF documents graphically. Figure 2-5 is an example created by IsaViz tools offered by W3C (World Wide Web Consortium).

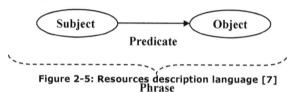

Figure 2-5: Resources description language [7]

According to Standard set forth by the World Wide Web Consortium (W3C), the data need to be stored based on RDF to implement Semantic Web. So they use RDF schema to model their storage process in a database. In fact, RDF schema determines the kind of relationship between data entry in order that a type of predicate is resulted by raw data that finally makes RDF meaningful, then we have no data but predicates which help us to obtain knowledge by their processing. RDF diagram class and RDF diagram property are determined in Figures 2-6 and 2-7, respectively. [41]

As mentioned, RDF predicates known as a term of RDF three words, have three parts : subject, predicate and object. In a three-word phrase, the subject is an example of an entity. [43] For example, in the entity of a student, a student named "Ali" is an example for this entity. Predicates are features of this specific entity where the object is values of these features. [43] You can see the RDF property diagram and RDF class diagram as follows. We make the example more complete: Suppose that a student's name is Ali. The sentence is mentioned as a three-word predicate: "Student 1, name, Ali". "Student 1" is subject and shows that we set forth an example of entity of student. "Name" is a predicate and determines that among the whole features, the adjective of "Name" with value of "Ali" has been important for us in this example. The data use the relational databases to store. [43] You can see this example in table 2-1.

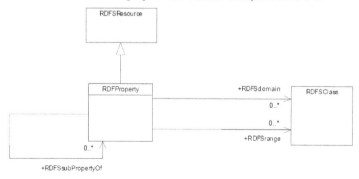

Figure 2-6: RDF Property diagram [41]

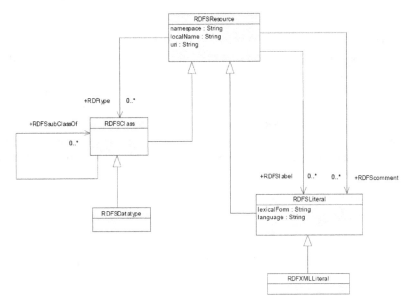

Figure 2-7: RDF Class diagram [41]

Table 2-1: Example for how to store RDF predicates in a relational database

Subject	predicate	object
Student 1	name	Ali
Student 1	age	25
Student 2	name	Amir

2-3-3 Programming and creating

To build and develop Semantic Web applications, programmers (developers) must collect and coordinate three various factors together [7]

- Programming language like Java or C #
- Semantic Web language like RDF and OWL
- Web protocols like HTML and SOAP

2-3-4 Make parameters smart in Semantic Web Applications

This section introduces the main parameters which play an important role to make Semantic Web sites smart. [8]

1. Browser Functionality

Web browser, the only user interface, can monitor the users behavior and follow their behavior.
- Web navigation
- Web Dynamic and Semantic Linking Hypertext Structures Functionality

2. Search Functionality

All internet users search for data to reach their needs. One of the other parameters drawn most attention of intelligent website designers and provided most effective algorithms is to use intelligent search system to reach a goal with no more time-consuming. Search was also examined from two directions:
• Intelligent search functionality
• Intelligent Semantic Query Expansion Functionality

3. Web functionality on different machines
The other parameter that attracted the attention of intelligent website designers was capable machines on different machines. The issue emerged after the portable PCs, PDAs and mobile phones were generalized.

4. Culture functionality
Users' culture and their web culture usage were the main effective factors. For example, opening a webpage with mother language on a user PC not only induces a close feeling and confidence in user, but also increases his/her self-confidence

5. Use of Multimedia Documents Functionality
Multimedia functionality can be used in intelligent Web Sites in three forms:
• Multimedia Handling Functionality
• Multimedia Metadata Functionality
• Multimedia Generation Functionality

6. Increase intelligent functionality
Designers found that when intelligent functionality increases, website content functionality also increases and they tried to change website content in such intelligently that they can increase users' satisfaction.

7. Semantic Growth Functionality
Semantic Growth was a mechanism that online marketers have called it as a promotion technique. This Semantic Growth has different types of activities based on two parameters of individual preference and sales of goods.

8. Ontology Functionality
Intelligent websites use Ontology in metadata application according to the organizational patterns. This is used by three forms.
• Ontology Schema Editor Functionality
• Ontology Instances Editor Functionality
• A combination of the two above

9. Different types of intelligent web applications
• Portal
• Ontology Tool
• Instance of Framework
• Semantic P2P Application
• Semantic Collaborative Tool

2-4 Web marketing

Philip Cutler, known as the father of modern management in the management literature, defines marketing as follows:

Marketing is a social and management process by which individuals and groups provide their needs and demands through the production, supply and exchange of useful and valuable goods with others. [46]

In the above definition, the *need* means no access to vital satisfaction; for example, people need home, food, health and recreation. In contrast, the *demand* means interest and tendency in some particular goods. For example, a hamburger sandwich or kebabs are products that may be desirable to meet food need. Marketing identifies unsatisfied needs and desires, according to Iran Park's marketing; it also defines and estimates the size of a defined market in addition to measure the level of profitability.

2-4-1 Marketing Components [1]

Marketing is based on four main categories (known as 4P) as follows:

• Product

• Place

• Pricing

• Promotion

Product is something sold by the businesses. The main features of these products are considerably important, but customers understanding of the product is called products "brand". It was along time that immediate delivery of goods and providing customer services at their needed time was envisioned by managers and officials. The category of Place and availability of goods and services was primarily very important for business. Although the Internet could not solve this problem, it has considerably helped in this area.

Price category is an amount that the customer pays for goods or services. In recent years, marketing experts have argued that businesses should think the price in a wider context.

The whole financial costs the customer pays for his/her desired goods must be mentioned in pricing category.

Three factors must be considered in *Promotion*:

• Message: What message does your business transfer?

• Media: newspapers, television, email, billboards, advertising on Internet sites

• Audience: people who are interested in your products or services.

2-4-2 Types of Marketing

Marketing include different types as follows:

• Industrial Marketing

• Consumption Marketing

• Multilevel marketing

• E-Marketing

Industrial marketing is defined as a group of business operations and practices which facilitates exchange processes between manufacturers and enterprise customers. Nature of industrial marketing can create value for customers by offering goods and services by which organizational needs are met and their goals are achieved.

In a comprehensive definition, industrial Marketing is the discovery process, translating the needs and demands of industrial customers and their requirements for specific products and services in order to effective relationship of distribute, pricing, after sales services, convince more and more customers for the continued use of these products and marketing services. This type of marketing differs from consumption marketing that can be mentioned as follows: 1) although both Industrial Marketing and Consumption Marketing need to know target markets, recognize market needs, design products and provide services to meet market needs, industrial marketing has a good management as compared to Consumption Marketing. Properties and features of products play an important role in industrial marketing and supplier who don't meet the desired customer demands won't be selected. As compared to consumption marketing, price plays a separate role in the industrial marketing. Sometimes industrial customers are willing to pay more money but receive on-time delivery and high quality goods and services, even in other cases such as purchase biddings, price is of great importance. The marketer must know that industrial goods demand emerged by end customer demand, i.e., product demand depends on how to use it in other products. Sometimes the marketer tries to stimulate end customer demand by promotion in order to increase demand for his/her industrial goods.

Multilevel marketing has more than eighty year's history. The earliest case of this type of marketing has been done by a bike seller in tsarian Russia. This event has been narrated by Yakov Sidorovich Perelman, an Russian mathematician lived in the early twentieth century to the late World War II, in "Live Mathematics" under a title of "cheap bike". In this way, buyers play the role of the marketer and they have to look for customer to reach the commission rather than professional marketers.

E-marketing is to use e-channels of customer relationship to spread the marketing message. [9]

In this case, internet marketing can be defined as "access to company objectives by meeting and exceeding customer needs better than competitors by using internet digital technologies. [10]

Internet marketing is to establish and keep mutual useful customer relationship by internet activities to facilitate products and service exchange in such a way that it achieve mutual goals. [11]

This definition includes the following sectors: process, establish and retain mutual useful customer relationship, Internet use to do marketing activities, exchange, achieve mutual goals. Moreover, online marketing refers to member companies of marketing logistics networks that contain a data flow of goods, services, experiences, payments and credits [10].

The starting point to gain success in e-marketing such as marketing or business strategy is to develop a strategic process containing a good definition in order to link marketing objectives by marketing relations and to design some methods to obtain desired objectives.

Cheston and Cheefe [12] and et al suggest that e-marketing strategy formulation should include elements and factors similar to traditional marketing strategy. To do this, you can use SOSTAC model by Paul Smith. The model includes following stages:

1. Situation analysis: Where are we now?
   - Situation analysis
   - Demand analysis
   - Customer Qualitative research
   - Competitor analysis
   - Collect information related to competitors
   - Intermediaries analysis
   - Marketing internal audit
   - Business effectiveness
   - Marketing effectiveness
2. Setting Goals: Where do we want?
3. Strategy formulation: how are we going to reach the desired Situation?

4. Tactics: What means to reach the desired state?

5. Performance: what plan do we have?

6. Control: Do we have achieved our goals?

2-4-3 Relational Marketing [13]

Relational marketing is a customer-oriented marketing. There is no goods promotion, products details, stimulation of customer feel to goods preference against various existing goods in market. The focal point is customer and the main factor is customer satisfaction. The satisfaction will cause customer confidence and loyalty for a business. The most important value is to retain customer relationship with business in relational marketing. This marketing has also changed its customer relationship due to improvement resulted by communications world, including Internet and mobiles. These developments have caused management to make and relationship with new communication tools differently than in the past. Their great impact is evident, because these tools include advantages to show relational marketing factors directly.

2-4-3-1 important factors in Relational marketing

• Customer Satisfaction

• Customer Retention

• Customer loyalty

• Customer Life Cycle

• Customer Life Time Value

• Customer Relationship Management (CRM)

Each of the above factors shows its importance in relational marketing typically. Notably to say, the relational marketing is a step behind in a business as compared to any other marketing practices. In other words, businesses plan to introduce their products, at first. This is natural. When business find some customers to their products, it goes to a relational marketing to reach their secondary target, i.e., eventually customer retention and loyalty. It is true that relational marketing set up lasts for a while, but it can be implemented based on the results of this type of marketing after all marketing policies were performed. As you see, the above three last factors are seeking for registering the events and customer reactions in relation to the business.

2-5 Customer Relationship Management (CRM) [7]

Customer relationship management refers to all processes and technologies which are used by companies and organizations to identify, encourage, develop, maintain and provide service to customers.

Organizations can shorten sales cycle and increase customer loyalty to establish closer relationships and revenue by using customer relationship management. CRM system can help retain existing customers and attract the new ones. Organizations use some techniques including customer relationship management, customer value analysis, corporate strategy and service mechanisms to improve customer relationship functionality. Customer relationship management is a strategy for attracting and retaining new customers. Operational customer relationship management includes all activities related to direct customers such as corporate.

Each activity in operational CRM is implemented by one of three operational corporate processes as follows: sales, marketing and service. While these processes are directly related to customer, analytical CRM provide all components needed to relation analysis and customer traits based on performance of operational CRM activities, emphasizing on customer needs and their exceptions .Before the organization can develop marketing or strategies of customer relationship management, they must understand how customers decide to buy. This decision process is called *Customer Buying Cycle (CBC)*.

Customer relationship management consists of three parts: customer, relationship, management. "Relationship" means the establishment of more loyalty and profitable customers by learner relationship and "management" means the creativity and guidance of a customer-oriented business and customer-centered in processes and corporate experiences.

2-5-1 History of customer relationship management [7]

It may be summarized the history of topics related to customer relationship management in the three periods as follows:

1. **Industrial Revolution (hand-to-the-mass production)** - One of the most important indicators is Ford's innovations to use mass production methods instead of hand product. Although changes in production methods caused to reduce the selection of customers in terms of product features (compared to the first category), products contained lower price resulted by new method. In other words, it was predicted that the most important objectives in selecting Ford's mass production method were to increase the efficiency and lower price.

2. **The Quality Revolution (mass production to continuous improvement)-** this period coincided with the innovations of the Japanese companies based on continuous improvement process. This in turn led to low production costs and higher quality products. When new methods of quality management such as TQM were introduced, this period reached its peak. Due to increase the competitive companies, expand the culture and keep or improve the quality (by different qualitative tools), competitive advantage won't be pioneer and useful anymore. And there is a need to find new ways to keep competitive advantages.

3. **Customer Revolution (continuous improvement to mass customization)-** Due to increase the expectations of customers, manufacturers were obliged to produce high quality in low cost and large variety. In other word, producer had to attract their attention to find some ways for satisfaction of their former customers.

2-5-2 Administrative challenges in customer relationship management

1. Lack of or inadequate customer relationship management strategy.
2. Opposition to users' compatibility with customer relationship management.
3. Debates about the correct management
4. Lack of business processes orientation
5. Inadequate support and training
6. Inappropriate use of technology

2-5-3 Advantages of customer relationship management

Customer relationship management is a tangible reality for business and has following advantages for the organizations:

1. Respond quickly to customer requests
2. Provide the condition for customer return
3. Reduce advertising costs
4. Increase marketing and sales opportunities

5. Deeper understanding of a customer

6. Receive customer feedback and develop current services and products

With regard to the benefits, there are several reasons for leading the organizations to capitalize on the customer relationship management:

1. Use current relationships with existing customers to maximize revenue growth

2. Identify, attract and retain the best customers

3. Introduce and define the more frequent sales procedures and processes.

4. Respond to the needs and meet customer demand

5. Create and implement an active marketing strategy that leads to reduce costs and deeper understanding of customers.

2-5-4 Gartner framework

Customer Relationship Management initiatives need a framework that ensures applications are strategic and integrated. Gartner has designed such an approach, which includes 8 steps:

1. Develop an effective organizational view requires corporate leaders to

• define customer relationship management for the institution.

• set the goals.

• draw a picture of what the organization wants to be for their target customers.

Target: it should have been created a distinct set of values that is important for customers.

2. Develop customer relationship management strategies

Customer relationship management strategy creates a view on how to establish a relationship with valuable customers and how to create loyalty to them.

Step One: Develop CRM strategy is to categorize the customers in groups, set the goals and criteria for each part.

Step Two: Evaluate the status of the customer base is an asset. It takes place in two dimensions by chart of customers' strengths and values.

• How much is the customer valuable to the organization?

• How much is the organization valuable for the customer?

3. Customer experience design

It should ensure whether organization products and interactions cause value for the customers, provide them continuously and obtain a good market. The operating feedback system increases the awareness of the organization about customer complaints and solves the related complaints.

4. Provide organizational cooperation

Organizational cooperation means as change the culture, organizational structures and behaviors to ensure that employees, partners and suppliers can work together to create value for customers.

5. Redesign of business processes

It is necessary to use the following framework to redesign of customer processes:

• Determine contact points and effective customer's processes, and draw their maps.

• Identify the key customer's processes, find the most unsatisfactory, and concentrate on them primarily.

• Determine and prioritize the processes based on their effects on the goal of customer relationships management.

• Apply the necessary changes in the organization (No process should be left without executive and official)
• Determine measurable or conceptual objectives using the customer's goals. Establish a customer service level agreement for each key process.
• Prioritize the processes based on their importance for customer and their effects on the goal of customer relationships management.

6. Develop customer Information Strategy
In this step, the correct data is collected and sent to the right place.

7. Use of Technology
In this step, data, customer applications, infrastructure and information technology architecture are managed.

8. Criteria
The internal and external indices of CRM success and failure are measured in this step. The indicator applications are as follows:

• set and measure the level of reaching in customer relationship management goals
• provide feedback to improve customer relationship management strategy and its implementation
• monitor the customer experience from organization
• change service staff compensation practice and given incentives
• assess organization for the competitors

In the final step, the goals that must be met and the tactics that should be used are defined.

2-6 Business process
Business process or method is set of related and structured activities that lead to provide service or products for one customer or specific customers along with the organizational objectives. Flow charts or diagrams display these processes in time order. [7]
Business process can be divided into three different categories: [7]
• *Management process*: business process management includes concepts, methods, and techniques for designing, monitoring, configuration, implementation and analysis of business processes. The processes involve people, organizations, systems and other information resources. Business process management has provided other abilities in addition to flow work automation. These abilities cause organizations to control more process. For example, a business process management can control the following processes:
  o Define and document the processes
  o Automate the implementation of processes
  o Identify opportunities and improve processes
  o Eliminate unnecessary activities
  o Control the performance of running processes
  o Cooperate the customers and partners in business processes
  o Reduce the needed resources
  o Increase coordination
  o Speed up the implementation of process cycle
  o Increase customer satisfaction
  o organizational agility

• **Operational processes**: It is the core of every trade and basis of creating the value flow. For example, operational processes include:
  o Manufacture
  o Sales
  o Marketing

• **Support process**: These activities support operational business processes. For example:
  o Accounting
  o Recruitment and human resources
  o Technical support

Business processes are determined by exact engineering of a business organization. Engineers can determine business processes by specifying organization framework, different sections of organization, the type and method of their relations, inputs, outputs and finally organizational objectives.

2-7 Data modeling

Data modeling is a method to identify and analyze the data required in the business or organization process. The required data are stored as an abstract model together with a specific definition. An actual implementation of an abstract model is called *a logical data model*. This implementation may require some logical data models. Data modeling not only provides a specific definition of the data, but also expresses the structure and its relationship. [27]

Data modeling techniques and methods are used for modeling the data to achieve resource management toward standardization, consistency and predictability. It is obvious to use standard modeling when we need to have a specific meaningful project. [28]

Data modeling strategy is part of the generation strategy of an information system that is defined as general and structured overview information systems. Information Engineering is of techniques that are used in this regard. [7] Data Modeling in Software Engineering is an abstract model to view and access to the data. [7] Data modeling is generally used to define data elements and its relationship. According to definition presented in the Mr. Heber-man book in 2009: data modeling is a way find for business and information technology experts who wants to interpret actual information by using set of words and symbol in order that they can improve internal corporate relationship and build software in fixed and flexible application flexible environment. [29] A data model explicitly interprets structure. Applications containing common data model have a database model, information system and also exchanging information procedure. Data models usually use a specific language. [30] There are two parameters in data named as "accuracy" and "relationship" that in turn they improve the importance of data for applications when to use them . Accuracy means that regulations relating to the data model can only be interpreted in one way, but not dull.[29]

Moreover, data modeling is a technique for database and needs of business process , that is why it was sometimes called "database modeling" because data modeling is implemented and created in database. [7]

By definition, various data models can be defined in following ways:

1. *Flat Model*: This cannot be clearly read as a data model. This includes a two-dimensional vector of data elements that all members of a column will contain the same values and communicate with all members of a line relate to each other. This model has been illustrated in Figure 2-8. [27.7]

	Route No.	Miles	Activity
Record 1	I-95	12	Overlay
Record 2	I-495	05	Patching
Record 3	SR-301	33	Crack seal

Figure 2-8: Flat Model [27]

Hierarchical Model: This model has tree structure in a way that each node is interpreted by a higher level node and storage time of each record includes nodes information of one line, as shown in figure 2-9. [7]

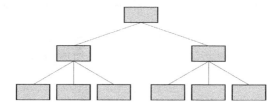

Figure 2-9: Hierarchical model [7]

2. *Network Model*: This model is specific mode of hierarchical model, as shown in figure 2-10, and the only difference is that each child node can have several father nodes.[27]

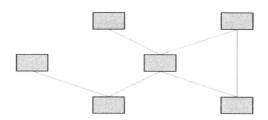

Figure 2-10: A network model [7]

3. *Relational model*: Data elements have been organized tabular in this model so that they can access and recover in different practices, while each table is independent of the other table.[27]

4. *Object-Oriented Model*: This model is quite similar to a relational model except that the objects (classes and their derivatives) are used instead of tables.

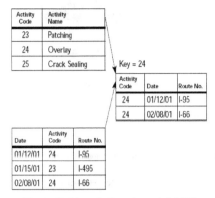

Figure 2-11: relational model [27]

5. Semantic data model: This is an abstract data model and needs abstract information. This means that this data will be interpreted differently. [31] Such a semantic data model indicates physical data store in a form used in real world, as shown in figure 2-12. [31]

There are two important tools for implementation of semantic data model: 1) XML schema and 2) RDF schema presented by World Wide Web Consortium in standard semantic web framework and they were summarized in chapter 2.

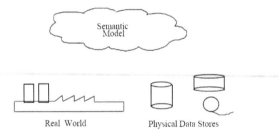

Figure 2-12: Semantic data models [7]

2-8 Process Modeling

Process modeling can be used in different fields. One application is the modeling of business processes. Process models are the core of process engineering concepts. Process modeling can be divided into different categories based on different point of view:

1. Classification by Coverage

The process modeling can be divided into five categories as follows:

- *Product-oriented:* The processes that lead to or provide a particular product. [32]
- *Decision- oriented*: a set of closely related decisions that lead to specific impact on business processes. [32]
- *Context-oriented*: sequence of texts in which the products have a major role in the process. [32]
- *Activity-oriented*: a set of related activities that lead to produce a specific product. [33]
- *Strategy-oriented*: In this model processes based strategies are considered. [34]

2. Classification by alignment [35]

This sort of process can be divided into three different categories:

- Strategic processes

- Tactical processes: processes that are designed to achieve the goal.
- Implementation processes: it is the lowest level of the process that speaks directly about how to implement the process.

3. Classification by Flexibility

Here if the model is designed based on the actual model and the ability to delete or modify the processes is very simple, we can say that the model is flexible.[35] As shown in figure 2-13, the method used in process modeling can be put in certain range of flexibility and influence low-high on it.[36]

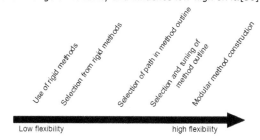

Figure 2-13: Classification by Flexibility [36]

But aside from the process modeling, model quality is important. The quality of a given process can be studied at three levels: [37]

1. Synthetic Quality: It measures the model consistency with rules and grammar used for modeling.
2. Semantic quality: It measures the level of model consistency with users need.
3. Pragmatic quality: It measure whether the model are adequately understood by all members associated with the modeling process or not.

2-9 User modeling

User modeling is subset of human resources interactions. It is the subject that researchers and designers have developed a model to identify users. It causes to predicate users problems their learning time. It is also a very low-cost method to test users. User modeling is a good guidance for user interface designers by which error rate and user learning time are reduced.

Results of users modeling are stored in computer systems in their user profile, so users' modeling content is developed by user profile. In each information system, user modeling is a process that is associated with systems analysis. Analyst engineers need users modeling to design the functionality as well as enter and exit the system depending on type and their interaction at best.

2-10 intelligent agents

Intelligent agent is an independent entity that acts and behaves depending on surrounding environment and according to a specific goal. [38] Intelligent agents can also use learning or knowledge to achieve the specific goal. These agents can be very simple or very complex.

Intelligent agents are usually interpreted schematically as an abstract application similar to computer programs that is why intelligent agents are sometimes called *Abstract Intelligent Agents*, in result there will be distinction between them and actual implementation in computer systems, biological systems, or organization. [7]

Intelligent agents are very similar to software interfaces. In computer science, the term intelligent agent is used instead of a software interface that is somehow smart, even if it is not rational agent. [38]

Intelligent agents are divided into 5 different classes based on the degree of intelligence and present ability: [38]

1. Simple reflex agents

These react against their current understanding. These agents are based on the condition rule. If condition then action. These agents are suitable when the environment is so totally identifiable that all the environmental conditions are identified.

2. model-based reflex agents

These agents can cover part of identifiable environment. These store current conditions and if the condition is repeated, they will repeat similar reaction. These recognize the environment by using this technique.

3. Goal-base agents

These agents are samples of *model-based reflex agents* that can store different information in the same conditions. Therefore, if the condition is repeated, they will have selectability among several reactions.

4. Utility-based agents

These agents can only detect between the goal and non-goal conditions. Optimum conditions can be measured by definition of a benchmark. This mechanism occurs at the intelligent agents, in result they enable to determine the best reaction.

5. Learning agents

These agents can work in unknown environments because they determine and learn the enviroment usinf trial and test, due to learning ability.

Intelligent agents have many applications. Some of these applications are discussed below. [44]

1. Intelligent agents' application in the Semantic Web
2. Intelligent agents' application in Web services and service-oriented computing
3. Intelligent agents' application in peer to peer (P2P) users' relationship
4. Intelligent agents' application in Grid computing
5. Intelligent agents' application in self-oriented management systems
6. Intelligent agents' application in complex systems
7. Intelligent agents' application in business software that generally provides sales and marketing service aiming at customer assistance, customer targeting and provide customer with information.

Clearly, these agents are all kind of software but their application varies. So it can be said that the implementation of an intelligent agents is only to implement software. Depending on the software requirements, the performance will be different.

This chapter briefly defined and interpreted some topics that existed in the research and will be used up to the end of the thesis. The next chapter will have overview of intelligence Web software produced from the last years to now.

Chapter 3
Overview of research conducted

As mentioned in section 2-1, E-commerce faced with many problems from 2000 to 2003 due to the recession. This problem led many projects, ideas and business models to be stopped and not to implement. Since 2003 then, due to the resolution of economic problems, business development and implementation of e-commerce business ideas led to revival of e-commerce. The implementation of e-commerce websites, semantic web, intelligent customer interactions with Web sites and searches were very interesting and thriving discussions. In this section, we plan to review the previous studies, so we study the literatures since 2003 then and describe intelligent website software. Then, we will discuss again "Make parameters smart in Semantic Web Applications" mentioned in section 2-3-4 and compare the web software based on intelligent parameters design, according to product year.

3-1 intelligent websites parameters
Intelligent Web Parameters are illustrated briefly in Table 3-1. We have used each number to refer to next sections.

Table 3-1: Intelligent Web Parameters [8]

Row	Functionality
1	Browse Functionality
1-1	Web navigation
1-2	Web Dynamic and Semantic Linking Hypertext Structures
2	Search Functionality
2-1	Intelligent Search Functionality
2-2	Semantic Query Expansion Functionality
3	Web functionality on different machines
4	Culture - Language functionality

5	Use of Multimedia Documents Functionality
5-1	Multimedia Handling Functionality
5-2	Multimedia Metadata Functionality
5-3	Multimedia Generation Functionality
6	Increase intelligent functionality
7	Semantic Growth Functionality
8	Ontology Functionality
8-1	• Ontology Schema Editor Functionality
8-2	• Ontology Instances Editor Functionality
8-3	• A combination of the two above
9	Portal web design
10	Use of Ontology Tool in web design
11	Use of Framework in web design
12	Semantic P2P Application
13	Semantic Collaborative Tools
14	Intelligent Wiki

3-2 Produced web software from 2003 to 2009

We study produced web software from 2003 to 2009, according to product year in Table 3-2 and compare each with intelligent parameters. The contents listed in Table 3-2 originate from resource [8] for 2003 to 2006 applications and resource [8] for 2007 to 2009 applications.

Table 3-2: Web software produced in different years [14, 8]

Row	Name of web software design in 2003	Intelligent Parameters
1	SEmantic portAL (SEAL)	1-2-4-9-11
2	Drug Ontology Project for Elsevier (DOPE)	1-2-5-9-11
3	SEmantic Collaboration (SECO)	1-2-9
4	Annotated Terrestrial Information (AnnoTerra)	1-2
5	Building Finder	1-2-5-9
6	Semblog	7-8-11-13
7	CS AKTive Space	1-2-4-5-6-9-13
8	Semantic Web for Earth and Environmental Terminology (SWEET)	----------------------
9	BioInformatics	----------------------
10	GeoShare	1-2-5-9
Row	Name of web software design in 2004	Intelligent Parameters
1	DBin	----------------------
2	MusiDB	1-2-7-9
3	The Multilingual Access to Data Infrastructures of the European Research Area (MADIERA) Portal	1-2-4-9
4	SWAP	----------------------
5	SemanticOrganizer	1-2-5-6-8-9
6	Platypus Wiki	1-2-8-9-14
7	MuseumFinland	1-2-3-5-7-9-11

Row		Intelligent Parameters
8	Knowledge Management Platform (KmP)	----------------------
9	pOWL	----------------------
10	Semantic Portal of International Affairs	1-2-3-4-5-9
11	Unspecified Ontology (UNSO)	2-8-10-12
12	Semantic Web Assistant	----------------------
13	Swoogle	----------------------
14	Flink	1-5-9
15	Bibster	1-2-6-8-9-11-12
16	Mediator EnvirOnment for Multiple Information Sources (MOMIS)	1-2-9-11
17	Annotea Shared Bookmarks	3-8-10
18	GOHSE	1-2-11
Row	**Name of web software design in 2005**	**Intelligent Parameters**
1	Pytypus	----------------------
2	Web Services Execution Environment	----------------------
3	DynamicView	1-2-4-5-9
4	Personal Publication Reader	1-2-8-9-11
5	Oyster	1-2-6-8-9-10-11-12
6	FungalWeb	2
7	CONFOTO	1-2-3-5-8-9
Row	**Name of web software design in 2006**	**Intelligent Parameters**
	There was no discussion at this year's special software and	
Row	**Name of web software design in 2007**	**Intelligent Parameters**
1	Freebase	1
2	Powerset	1-2
3	Twine	1-5-13
4	AdaptiveBlue	1
5	Hakia	2-8
6	TrueKnowledge	2
7	Clear Forest	1-4-5-6
8	Spock	2
Row	**Name of web software design in 2008**	**Intelligent Parameters**
1	Yahoo! SearchMonkey	1-2
2	Powerset (acquired by Microsoft in 2008)	2
Row	**Name of web software design in 2009**	**Intelligent Parameters**
1	Google Search Options and Rich Snippets	2-4-9
2	BBC's Semantic Music Project	1-5-6-12
3	Glue	1-12

After expressing produce web software from 2003 to 2009 together with intelligent parameters, we have decided to explain more about some of them.

3-2-1 SEmantic portAL (SEAL) – 2003

The core of this software was designed in 2002 [15, 8] aiming at use of an ontology to Web management and its portal. In this ontology, there was a relationship between different sources. In addition, when information schema is used, control navigation will be possible. But the software was not only conceptual framework in 2003. This framework was improved and became a framework for integrating knowledge. This framework was presented in five abstract layers 5 which are shown in Figure 3-1. [8, 16]

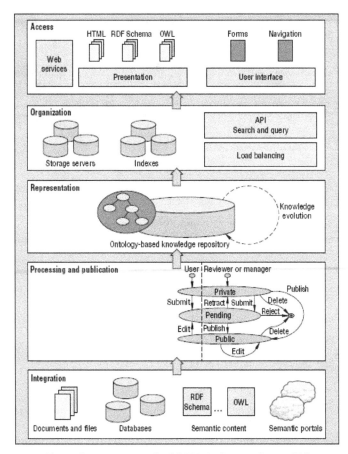

Figure 3-1: Framework of SEAL 5 abstract layers [8]

As you can see in Figure 3-1, knowledge of the first layer which is the bottom layer (integration) moves to the highest layer i.e. access layer. The integration layer consists of several modules, each of which is able to communicate with a specific type of the data. Some methods are provided for knowledge processing in second layer. An instance of the content is created in this layer. The third layer or so-called representation layer shows knowledge by using the ontology and the knowledge representation languages such as RDF Schema and OWL. Some methods are presented for indexes and search in fourth layer or organization layer. Finally in the fifth or so called access layer, some methods view content in different but integrated way. [8, 16]

3-2-2 Drug Ontology Project for Elsevier (DOPE) – 2003

In this application, access to reference data from multiple life sciences is possible through an innovative user interface. This user interface offers a search system based on the terms that follow automatic index structure, RDF-based query and concept-based visualization. The overall architectural design of the software is illustrated in Figure 3-2. [17, 8]

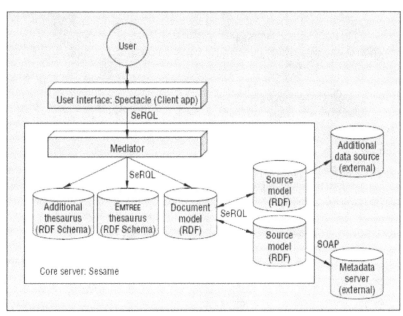

Figure 3-2: Schematic of DOPE software architecture [8]

This interface leads the users to search and represents the structured search result. It offers user query and navigation clearly. Moreover, it can interact to users by using Sesame exchange and query language and infrastructure between information resources, Thesaurus representation and external document metadata using RDF implementation [18, 8]

3-2-3 DBin – 2004

Dbin is a platform for Semantic Web peer to peer relationship. Indeed, it has used Semantic Web features and advantages to enable users to interact with existing intelligent backup files and media. DBin is combination of experimental units that work to specific instances of metadata such as user interface (extract audio metadata, textual data analysis, and desktop integration). It can inhibit unwanted information by using politics of personal trust. [19, 8] DBin architecture can be seen in Figure 3-3.

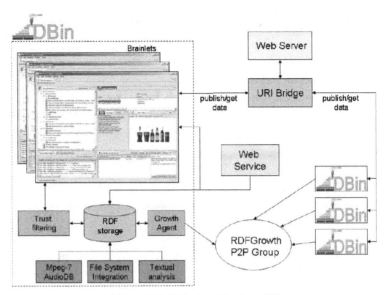

Figure 3-3: DBin Architecture [8]

In this architecture:

• All data is stored in the database using RDF.

• A set of modules are used to communicate with the database.

• The algorithm called RDFGrowth is used to collect the RDF metadata from others to identify common interests.

• The interesting and attracting point is that DBin only works in a certain range.

3-2-4 Personal Publication Reader (PPR) – 2005

PPR is an example of a Personal Reader Framework. [20, 21, 8] The framework provides a model of design, implementation and maintenance to Personal recommendations and contextual information. [20, 21, 8]

This content can provide information list in reader section and personal recommendation plus contextual information in personalization section for its users. PPR is a web framework with below web services using data mining, arguing ontology-base knowledge, describing metadata and providing intelligent view [8,21,20]

User Interface construction

• An interface between user applications and provided personal services

• User modeling

• Provide personalization capabilities

As it can be seen in Figure 3-4, PPR describes simultaneous the personalization and representation of distributed data on the Web. This software includes four executive stages[22]

• Data Collection

• Implementation: it is to extract update data.

• The argument: use of argument rules to semantic description generation and knowledge base such as ontology and user properties.

• User Interface generation: a convenient and personalized user interface is generated using the result of previous stage and RDF language.

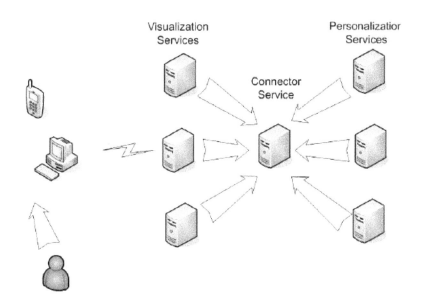

Figure 3-4: PPR Architecture Framework [8]

3-2-5 Plan presented in 2007

In this section we examine a proposal in 2007 which was presented by a student in his dissertation. He concludes briefly through studding above mentioned software from 2003-2006 that: [8]

2003: It is better that software are integrated in two asymmetrical field 1) XML data 2) Information resources where software designers have not considered such a thing in design.

2004: it mentions the benefits of user interface capabilities have been implemented by the Semantic Web languages .

2005: it uses ontology, Schema and model for design and implement for produced software.

Finally it is concluded that any information system, data collection, storage and processing is necessary. Thus use of processing results to represent suitable end users is very important. Data collected by the information system called metadata. Metadata should be involved in four operational phase. He offers four phases of operational metadata under metadata transfer process as shown in Figure 3-5.

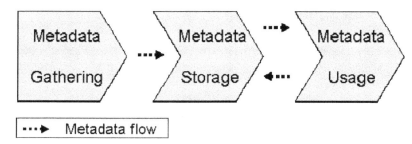

Figure 3-5: The process of metadata flow [8]

• Phase I: metadata gathering
• Phase II: metadata storage

• Phase III: metadata usage

• Phase IV: metadata flow between the three operational phase

As illustrated in figure 2-10, metadata flow is right–to-left movement in information system but the use of metadata storage is an idea to express that use of metadata lead to generate new metadata.

Metadata gathering is of great importance because decision for end user (to have a semantic web) is made by Metadata gathering.

Metadata transfer process is mentioned as the most basic information route on the proposed framework in his thesis. The interesting subject in his thesis is software design relationship and proposal framework to have a semantic web.

Software architecture is shown by a document or diagram. [8] The document or diagram does not meet the whole software designer need. According to his theory, he confirmed the "4 +1" View Model of Software Architecture that was proposed to software architecture by Conallen in 1999. But he expresses a different view to name of this architecture. Figures 3-6 and 3-7 illustrate Conallen architecture.

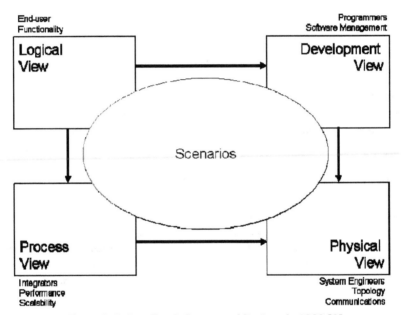

Figure 3-6: Conallen Software architecture in 1999 [8]

As shown is figure 3-6 , model of Conallen software architecture consist of 4 views and each view describe a separate subject in software design . These four views include:

• Logical view: it mainly represents the software requirements performance.

• Processing view: it is responsible for synchronization and concurrency of the design parameters.

• Physical view: it is responsible for the adaptation of hardware and software design, and vice versa is the later.

• Development view: it describes a static organization of software in a development environment.

And finally the scenario: it is described by using an architecture scenario. He changes the above model as follows:

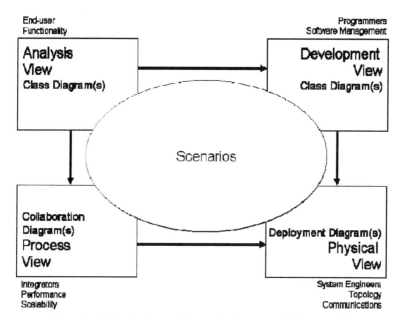

Figure 3-7: The implementation of software architecture [8]

In this thesis, it is describe that:

Analysis view: Analysis is a logical view shows application needs and is represented as object-oriented diagram class.

Processing view: some software unapplied needs such as performance and availability are expressed here, and are illustrated by interactive diagrams such as protracted ones. [8]

Development view : it concentrate on make software modular. It is done depending on internal enterprise needs and related software.

Physical view: the distribution scalability and other part of non-functional needs are represented in this view using Deployment diagram.

Finally the scenario: scenario outlined in the proposed architecture is based on four basic factors that are shown in Figure 3-8. These four factors include: [8]

• Semantic Web Challenge requirements
• Analysis of Semantic Web Applications domain
• Metadata transfer process
• The controversialist about the Semantic Web stack architecture or semantic web architecture

In 2007, the student concluded that there should be software design architecture and a scenario for describing the architecture in order to have intelligent web. According to his thesis, an intelligent web scenario is described in such a way that needs and suitable software for a intelligent web should be identified and implemented based on semantic web architecture, besides metadata have an important place in complete intelligent applications. There are four views in software design architecture that are interpreted at above.

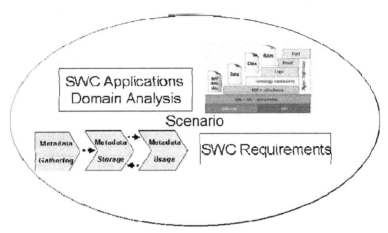

Figure 3-8: General scenario of proposed architecture [8]

3-2-6 Proposed Plan in 2008

This section studies other proposed plan that was written in 2008. [23] Here, a framework has been indicated for semantic web to operate in industry and business. The authors of the proposal study necessity and principles for a Semantic Web framework in business and offer their framework. They begin to discuss that value to have an intelligent web is not clear for businessmen because they have no view about its importance and technology. Therefore, they rarely decide to invest on intelligent web in their business. It is disappointing that when most of them having a large experience and skill in their job decide to enter the web and participation, they have no intelligent web framework. In contrast, the experienced human in computer sciences and technology has no view and experience in business and commercial sciences. Thus, to have intelligent web in business and preferably to have a good and prosperous idea for setting up e-commerce, there should be three major principles .The importance of these three principles together is so that are shown in figure 3-9.

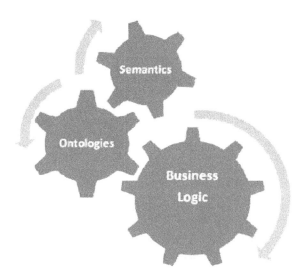

Figure 3-9: Semantic Web Triple approaches in Business [23]

They continue to express that each business should make clear 2 subjects before to implement its e-commerce, including:

•The overall performance of internal business processes

• Strengthen the institutional networks and the exploit business power in connection with their market, partners and other independent businesses

In summary, as software engineering and analysis is necessary for implementing and designing computer software, business identification and performance externally and internally are also of a great importance. These two cause to improve organizational goals to have a successful e-commerce.

Then four layer analysis of the engineering are examined determining business logic place in Semantic Web framework. As shown in figure 3-10, these four layers are:

Data layer: When we deal with information systems, core component of the system consists of data that are related to services and products.

Semantic Web and ontological engineering layer: necessary engineering principles for a Semantic Web are expressed in the layer.

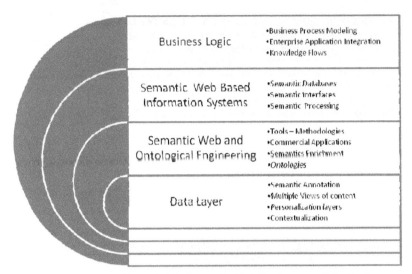

Figure 3-10: Semantic Web Text approach in Business

Semantic Web based information systems layer: the main target is to integrate semantic web components in application framework.

Business logic layer: it aimed at understanding the business with all the features, components and objectives. Finally it presents its framework, after mentioning necessary details and arrangements, as shown in figure 3-11

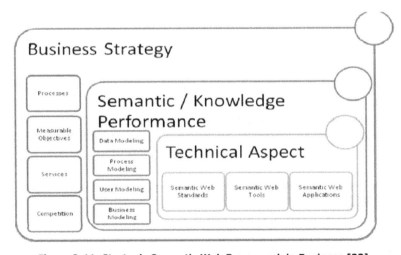

Figure 3-11: Strategic Semantic Web Framework in Business [23]

As you can see, the framework has three original layers. Innermost layer is related to the Semantic Web. Outermost layer is related to commercial firms engineering that shows knowledge requirement of business processes. The middle layer, the main objective of the framework, is related to necessary parameters to comply with the semantic Web and business principles.

The proposed framework is assessed by two factors EAI (Enterprise Application Integration) and complexity. EAI-level has been considered a proper scale for the measurement and evaluation of framework because it mentions the level of information, services and enterprise business. In principle, this measure determines whether the implementation of Semantic Web technique is based on the organizational principles or not.

An interesting point in this model is to model the customer and business in the middle layer.

1. One of authors of the above proposed plan implements Rhizomer as an active platform for customer interaction on semantic web in 2008 that implements user interface data and its flow in information system so intelligent that identifies end user feeling as semantic web intelligent interaction by using the resulting implementation. [24] Techniques for storing, processing and viewing the final processing the gathering data are mentioned in the software. The used data in the software are metadata that were transferred to information system by end user. The important parameters in software design include: 1) customer-oriented design and 2) The ability to delete and edit metadata by users. The main idea of the software in metadata processing is to categorize their graph based on the subject. Explaining the above mentioned algorithm is out of the thesis, but for more information and study, you can refer to his article. [24] The most important factor of software to have an intelligent interaction is to use Semantic Web Query Language.

3-2-7 Use of Intelligent agent

Apart from the above, intelligent agent is another mechanism used to make smart the websites. As previously noted in the section 2-10, intelligent agents have different applications. One of these applications is to use the software in commercial software, especially for commercial websites.

Use of intelligent agents in commercial software has a wide stand in different areas of the business. [48]

Use of intelligent agents in commercial software can be for some purposes including 1) *Sales and marketing* (targeted customers, customer assistance, providing appropriate promotions, provide appropriate information to customer) 2) *Banking services* (e-banking services) 3) *Communications* (smart phones, human-computer relationship) 4) *Export systems* (control rules, translation services, providing customers services) [48]

3-3 Current worldwide websites

In all above mentioned, there is no name of successful worldwide business websites. The main reason is that none of them was pioneer in intelligent web method, but they are innovative and pioneer in presenting web business model. Indeed, they have used intelligent techniques as a proposed and efficient method in some fields. We mention some worldwide websites and express their successful reason in e-commerce.

1. eBay: The most important success factor for the company is to implement auction business model on the website. But after implementing the business model, eBay was one of pioneers in providing a secure and reliable electronic payment service to customers in the world of e-commerce. This website's success can be divided into the following factors: [49]

- Created automation in sales technique especially the unique items
- Reliability in online payment method
- Easy to work with websites for different types of customers
- provided services in addition to sales techniques
- World website
- Regional variation
- successful advertising

EBay benefits from intelligent agent in sale , electronic payment, services and advertising.

2. Amazon: This is a customer-oriented Website so that it coddles its customers. The main technique is to try to achieve customer need. The website tries to do it by customer navigation control. Besides, it also offers effective advertising that is based on previous purchases and relationship between the current customers with previous ones. Amazon does all the things through an intelligent agent. [49]

3. Dell: this Company could achieve successful e-commerce by implementing the personalization for the orders of customers.

4. Yahoo: The success of this site is due to all internet services that are provided as a portal to customers. The services include providing free news service, information services, online advertising, sports news, music and video clips. [49]

Wit regard to previous studies we found that making smart the websites is an interesting category. The importance is evident in business websites. We plan to present a concept to design the business website which has customer interaction and intelligent contents. E-commerce websites interaction is an important issue for which no method has been presented in the previous studies. As mentioned before, it is obvious that customer enters to a business website as potential customer in any place and time but website is responsible to convert potential customer to actual one. Therefore, intelligent website-customer interaction that led to simulate real physical world interaction in virtual world will improve customer conversion ability , influence on customer relationship , and have direct results in his/her loyalty and confidence. The effect of customer loyalty and confidence that led to frequent referrals is the most important factor whereby each business thinks about its customer relationship. Thus, the sciences of customer relationship management are very important and influential. Although it attempts to increase web attractiveness, easy work to web sites for customers, the missing piece is use of customer relationship management in web sites. As previously mentioned in Chapter 2, customer relationship management should be done at the customer's arrival time. So, we are looking for establishing an intelligent website in which mutual customer-website interaction begins intelligently in the website. Web content tries to identify the customer using an intelligent agent experienced in customer relationship management and continues its management to complete web customer process.

Chapter 4

Proposed Model

The ultimate goal of this thesis is to create an intelligent customer relationship management (CRM). CRM is a strategy that business uses to improve customer loyalty, obtain new customers, lower the costs, control all pre- and post- shopping activities and finally integrate programs and schedules. [46] On the other hand, CRM is known as an information system because such applications primarily store customer's data and then analyze and do processing them. The processing results are used in the implementation of marketing processes and establishment of customer relationship management. [46]

As it is clear from the title of the thesis, we want to offer a way to create an intelligent CRM in e-commerce. As also noted in Chapter 2, the only interface between businesses and customers in e-commerce is the website. The customer information is collected solely by the interface. Regarding previous studies, each website client should be looked as a potential customer. All the facilities provided and the content is identical for all clients. One of the most important issues in websites that have been ignored is no difference in the website content of any client. Truly, it is impossible to identify the client at arrival time. Please note that all tools and techniques are used to design and implement intelligent websites are only to improve website functionality. [1] Intelligent web is defined in intelligent user services, for example intelligent search is a tool presented to clients to get a prompt and target results. This causes to increase web functionality and attracts customer satisfaction. The missing piece which shows client cognition is missing. As illustrated in figure 4-1,

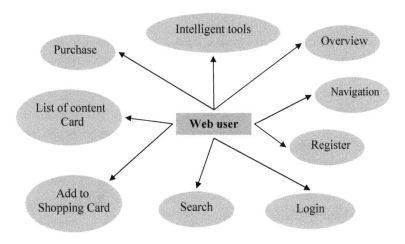

Figure 4-1: Current World Wide Web by users

Visiting the web worldwide, we understand that client register is optional, if the client decides to purchase from the web site, he/she should enter a series of personal information in related forms. For example, name, surname, email address and the Bank account specification. If the client doesn't decide to buy, the website is not a business website for him/her but it will be a very good information website that can use existing facilities to obtain needed information.

How can have a business website but are unable to attract potential customers? What happens to this great business that causes to make a big difference between a real shop and virtual store? The answer is very simple. The interesting discussion in the real world is buyer - seller interaction or in other words, presence human sense in the business. In e-commerce virtual world, there are no five human senses. Due to lack of senses, there is no mutual understanding. So we posed the question: how can such a sense of human simulate in virtual world? Human can establish relationship together by talking, so the relationship can be simulated by developing a website interaction and attempting to collect a series of client information in which induces a type of close feeling in client and then can reach to main goal i.e. identify the client. One of the advantages client interactions is that even if they refer to website to use existing information, it can convince the customer to buy by specific marketing techniques and information arising from the interaction after finishing the activity.

Therefore, the aim is to present an intelligent content management on e-commerce websites in terms of relationship and interaction simulation in the physical real world by which we can improve level of cognition and interaction for an intelligent customer relationship management. To reach an intelligent content management in e-commerce website, it should introduce an intelligent semantic web design model whereby interacts with its users (customer) in user interface (webpage) in order that can collect needed information and indicate their effects on a given content.

In previous chapter, we understood that many websites were designed and produced under the title of intelligent web with different frameworks. As mentioned before, many different policies were introduced along with making smart the websites such as create an intelligent search, register user event and navigation, use of ontology in software design, use of metadata in different way and etc. But none of them can meet our need to present an intelligent content management. In next section, we study the framework to implement semantic web applications to meet our needs.

4-1 Proposed Model

Now we will describe our proposed model as shown in Figure 4-2. The principles mentioned in proposed plan in 2008 fully comply with fundamentals of business intelligent website design. We make the ability to create an intelligent content management on user interface possible by following changes in order that we can simulate existing interaction of the real business world in e-commerce virtual world , and finally we get an intelligent customer relationship management.

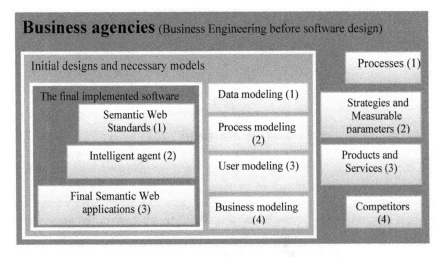

Figure 4-2: Framework of proposed model

4-2 Plan Details

In this section we will explain more about the proposed framework and the necessary definitions.

4-2-1 Business agencies engineering before software design
4-2-1-1 Business process

Business process was explained in details in Sections 2-6.

4-2-1-2 Measurable parameters

In business, measurable parameters are called those exist in the business activities and are used to improve businesses. For example, a new strategy design is resulted by changing criterion. The said criterion must be measured after implementing to determine success value in used method. These parameters arise and are evaluated during the implementation. Measurable parameters are different in every business.

4-2-1-3 Products and Services

Products and services differ in each business. Businesses offer products and services depending on target determined in meeting customer (s) needs. Products and services are produced, provided and supported during business process.

4-2-1-4 Competitors

In each market, there is much competition for any business. It is very important to keep business life, gain success and enable to compete. Each business must identify its competitors in market and recognize the used strategies in order to compete with them.

4-2-2 Initial designs and necessary modeling
4-2-2-1 data modeling

Data modeling was described briefly in section 2-7. Based on details and requests, we need a semantic data model for proposed model, and then the necessary database for needed data storage must be a semantic database.

4-2-2-2 process modeling

Process modeling was fully defined in section 2-8.

4-2-2-3 user modeling

User modeling was fully defined in section 2-9.

4-2-2-4 Business modeling

Business processes Management means to design implement and improve the functional activities that link individual, information systems, and the trading partners. Any modeling is created to easy understanding of entity, therefore business modeling is also done in this way. With regard to technologies improvement, use of information technology (IT) tools as well as modeling (by tools), it is possible to simulate model process, and it can easily show existing channels in the organization. Corporate engineering is impossible without using modeling and simulation tools, with regard to complexity of existing corporate process and their relationship. Notably to say, the business complexity will be increased by passing times; in result, the process will be more complex. [7] Therefore there is no difference between business modeling and business process modeling [40]. This package in the middle layer means to implement business process model that has been designed by analysis engineers in previous layer.

4-2-3 Final implemented software
4-2-3-1 Semantic web standards

In structure and web design, Web standards means instructions, rules and technical specifications determined by Web World Wide Consortium that indicates and describes general form and all aspects of web world network, s it was spoken in chapter 2.

4-2-3-2 Semantic Web Applications

Final implemented software is the ultimate goal of the Semantic Web is a Semantic Web project.

4-2-3-3 Intelligent agent

Intelligent agent has been offered in proposed framework due to ability to create intelligent user interaction, web content management and finally know and gather the needed information for customer relationship management. Three main tasks of the agent were identified. Users mean the website visitors. By definition, the intelligent agent places among the intelligent software. Clearly after receiving user information, the agent must identify and manage them. Users can be different in terms of parameter. Since the second function of intelligent agent is web content management for each separate user, so similar condition is unbelievable because all human vary individually unless otherwise shared conditions are defined and they are known similar regardless of differences. On the other hand, users were modeled in this software system but their profile that determines main criterion of user performance is fixed and non-predefined .according to above mentioned, the proposed intelligent agent is in model reaction class.

1. Create an intelligent interaction: The intelligent agent must create capability of publish, query, browse, edit and interact for the website users. [24] But what manner of interaction should be provided and what is important in this interaction? Interaction aims at creating a series of query by intelligent agent. Several targeted questions are asked the customer in order to obtain needed information. Any business needs different information depending on type of its activity and certain customers. The differences in the understanding of business processes and customer recognition are identified by analyst engineers and finally are modeled. So the intelligent agent asks some targeted questions to gather information, using business model and user model. Obviously, all needed information cannot be achieved in the first visit, so they should be categorized and arranged based on their importance and question order in different time cycle. User profile is stored in profile of information systems. This profile must enable to expand because new information is added to it in every visit. Data stored in the profile are divided into two main categories.

A) The basic profile of each user is required. The basic profile includes name, surname, age, gender, education, e-mail address and so on.

B) The profile is achieved by user navigation on the site. Each web user makes use of existing facilities on the websites. Navigation, search, click on existing links and the others are proposed to semantic web clients and intelligent agent can gather needed information of client by using and managing the above abilities. User profile is defined as shown in figure 4-9.

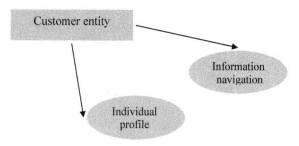

Figure 4-3: User Profile

To have a good semantic web performance, it should be possible to establish a relationship with set of structured information and presumption rules in order to benefit from an automatic argument method. [39] The user interface must use query language for his/her interactions in semantic websites. [24] To use a language, the data structure, organization and process must be determined in order that a proper language can be selected. Since business processes, organizational and users' performance are all modeled in our proposed framework, ontologies are designed. Thu, the best language for establishing the intelligent agent interaction is Ontology Web Language (OWL). [25] According to standard set forth for semantic websites, data structure is defined based on RDF. As noted in Section 2.3.2, data are not raw but also they are predicated. This predicate can be deduced from the needed knowledge. That's why the needed database for data storage should be designed based on the RDF Schema. The RDF and OWL (Resource Description Functionality) interprets briefly data structure and semantic relationship with a simple program, respectively. [45]

2. The second function of the user interface is web content management that begins after establishing client interaction. In the software interface must enable to change the content presented to clients while gathering the needed information depending on obtained information. This intelligent agent must enable to change customer web content depending on receiving data from him/her, using tools as data mining and semantic website tools. For example, after it knew user age, it should change the advertising based on his/her age. Or if a client clicked on a particular item, it should change its ads strategy according to specific marketing techniques such as User Base or Item Base. The created content management is a very important step in further understanding the customer because the customer interacts against the changes and the feedback will lead to a greater understanding of client. These changes can be made based on two techniques. 1. Arguments that intelligent agent it can obtain by existing data processing with RDF standard in the database. 2. Data mining. in marketing that is the most basic principles of business processes , data mining techniques is used for two specific marketing techniques. The first technique is to classify customers using Clustering algorithms. The clustering is very important in the advertising because specific customers see only the desired advertising or do specific decision. In other word, a certain management can be created in the offered content. The second technique is to use classification algorithms. Using classification algorithms, decision tree can be created and considerable type of new clients' behavior can be predicted accordingly. Here, we don't plan to talk about details and determine the optimal algorithms because it is beyond the scope. In deed, we can have a needed knowledge to change and data collection simultaneously, using the tools. When we created an intelligent interact, identified client, and established an intelligent content management, we can develop our result in personalization of website, using information received by the

customer. Client sees intelligent website resulted by his/her cognition . Here we could simulate real buyer-seller interactions in virtual world.

3. Today, with regard to mass production of the goods, and improved supply-demand ratio services, producers must attract customer satisfaction and it is impossible to define market and supply based on past limited tools. Experience has shown that organizations with traditional view toward customer concepts, product, market, sales, purchase, competition, promotion, quality and etc. have lost their capital and success. With the emergence of a competitive economy, concepts like customer-oriented and customer satisfaction are considered the foundation of business and any organization that pays no attention is removed from the market. Each organization has administrative classification, organizational charts, different sections , objectives, policies, instructions and many others; large organization and different section not only is not important for the customers ,but also needs someone to solve their problem and meet their needs. . [51] The customer-oriented organization aims at meeting the most valuable requests of customer and it believes that customer satisfaction is its capital and ensures its return of investment. The caption of thoughts and planning is to provide customer services. [52] Real criterion for value of an organization is customer satisfaction, according to society and owners and without it , no company can survive , create a job, provide the needs of people works and service s for them. A customer-oriented organization cannot reach to success without making a suitable relationship with customers. Moreover, in modern world known as a quality-oriented and customer-oriented world, customer-oriented and customer-based are infrastructures of economic and business activities. Customer relationship management Customer relationship management emphasizes on the value exchange between customer and the organization and value making in this relationship. Therefore, attempt of organizations to develop long term relationships with customers based on creating value for both sides is the main goals is customer relationship management. In other words, the aim of customer relationship is to give advantages through mutual benefit exchange and do obligations and commitments . Customer relationship management is business strategy that is improved by technology development by which companies establish a beneficial relationship based on received and perceived optimal value of the customers.[53] Kaplan and Norton believe that customer aspect is the most important aspect in measuring the organization performance, and Peters and Waterman have expressed that identification of customer needs is feature of successful organization and systemically study and quality of customer satisfaction and loyalty is the most important health indices. Four aspects of customer requirements include:

• Knowledge of results (objectives of using services) or the ways and means to achieve results
• exact determination and description of customer needs
• customer participation in a first time possible
• expectations of the consumer (customer) service.

If it is supposed to provide a quality or service, it is necessary to make a balance between customer expectations and what can be offered.

Today, manufacturing or service organizations consider customer satisfaction as a important criterion for assessing the quality of their work and this trend is still rising. Customer care and satisfaction refer to compete globally. Blanchard and Galovin believe: customer satisfaction is resulted by perceive of the customer during a deal or value relationship so that the price is equal to customer quality- price ratio. [51] Definition of customer satisfaction accepted by many of experts is as follows: customer satisfaction is a result gained by comparing the expected performance of customer before purchase to real perceived performance and paid cost. [26]

According to marketing literature, customer satisfaction has two exchange and general dimensions. The exchange concept of customer satisfaction is related to customer evaluation of any purchases. The general concept of customer satisfaction is related to consumer evaluation and general feeling about the whole attitudes and their purchases of the brand. In fact, it can be said that general dimension of customer satisfaction is a function of all the satisfaction or non- satisfaction in his previous transactions. Customer general (overall) satisfaction is overall evaluation of experience of buying and consuming a good or service in a long period of time. The overall satisfaction is a better index for performance in the past, present and future of the company.

In fact, customer relationship management is a strategy for gathering needs and business behavior of customers that lead to make a stronger relationship between them. Finally, a strong customers relationship with is the key to success in any business. Many technologies were presented in form of CRM but the CRM view as a set of technology is incorrect. To have a better understanding of CRM, it is considered as a process that assists us to gather various information about customers, sales, effectiveness of marketing activities, customer respond rate and market trends and needs . The main idea of CRM is to help businesses obtain a better view toward business and values that each customer causes for organization, using the technology and human resources. If a customer relationship management system can act in accordance with the above idea, the organization will be able to provide better service to customers. With this proposal, with an intelligent customer interaction, in fact, we could also do customer relationship management cleverly. When we reach to abstract customer cognition (website clients), then we can have our intelligent customer relationship management through different marketing techniques such as relational marketing.
.

4-3 Suggested parameters for evaluating the proposed model

If a website design framework is considered based on business principles and finally a customer relationship management are created, then evaluation criterion can not only be software parameters. Although a website is designed and implemented by principles of software engineering and user visits it to do business, software engineering criteria are not only important. Here we introduce 2 other parameters (in addition to previous parameters) to evaluate our proposed framework that evaluate designed website in terms of business. The mentioned parameters include:

4-3-1 conversion rate

Conversion rate was defined in details in Chapter 2. The higher a Web site conversion rate is the more satisfied customers toward website performance shows. Since the framework is an intelligent web design framework, so the conversion rate is a parameter showing the value of implemented project for that business. Each business agency that creates a new business model can satisfy the new model when i.e. more income move to main goal and it is not obtained unless it can attract more customers and meet their satisfaction and finally reach a lasting and sustained buying. E-commerce is a new business model.

4-3-2 Customer Life time value [13]

This parameter was one of the most important factors described in section relational marketing in Chapter 2. We define it here and explain the reason why it was mentioned as evaluation parameter for proposed framework.

Life time value is number value indicates duration or interval time of customer visit against previous visit. This value is different depending on the business activities of enterprises. Or in other words, Life time value of customer for each business is different. For example, a customer can refer to a supermarket every day and purchase daily needed items, but he/she may go to bookstore every month and purchase book.

The reason why this parameter is considered to evaluate proposed framework is that business agencies can measure their customer satisfaction from website performance, because satisfaction makes them to return at due time. The continuing satisfaction will effect on customer retention and loyalty and this is what the business expects the customer. One of the most important factors that may effect on enhancing this parameter is the customer relationship management.

Chapter 5
Providing a case study

In this chapter we provide an example to elaborate the mentioned studies in detail. For example, we have an online store. The store is analyzed based on framework we proposed in the previous chapter. Implementation of the software would be expensive in terms of time, technical, human resources and resources so we only mention the topics of theory and design details. As noted in the previous chapter, implementation of business web sites under the proposed framework is operational in three distinct phases.

5-1 Shop Engineering before software design
5-1-1 Business process
1. **Supply**: at first, business store supply merchandise to offer customers. This product is supplied in any way possible. For instance, whether they purchase the good from one or more suppliers or produce by themselves. In the first case, provide the necessary goods means to purchase them and to produce them in the second. In the second case, cycle of production of goods is among the activities of store.
2. **Sales**: The next activity after the supply of goods is to sell them. Sales process can be divided into several smaller activities. For example, advertising, pricing, marketing, accounting and so on.
3. **Provide after-sales service:** Each store is obliged to provide after-sale services to buyers. These services are different. Service type is characterized by Goods itself. For example, if the product is a kind of home appliances, then carry it to home; installation, commissioning and training on how to use it are set of services offered to customers.
4. Each store has some intra-organizational activities in addition to the above mentioned. Or in other words, it does not relate directly to goods and customer. They have indirect relationship such as employment of human resources, management, and transportation and so on.

5-1-2 Strategies and measurable parameters
Store strategies are the most activities that specify how to overcome the competitors. Thus, store goals primarily must be determined in order to know store programs for implementation of strategies, in result the proper analysis will obtained when implementing e-commerce model. Measurable parameters are the parameters that change when implementing the considered programs and strategies. In other word, there are parameters that change new strategies and planning such as the percentage of loyal customers. This percentage will change by implementation of a new strategy and the low or high level can determine strategy success.

5-1-3 Products and Services
It includes all products and services that are offered by a shop. In this example we consider no specific commodity.

5-1-4 competitors

Every business needs to know its competitors in the market and needs to know their policies, strategies to be able to compete with them.

5-2 Initial designs and necessary modeling

5-2-1 Data Modeling

As noted in section 4-2-2-1, the data model should be designed for applications under the proposed framework; it must be semantic data model. Semantic data model should be based on schema RDF. To model the data, the data existed in the store must be identified. By analysis of store and determining the entities and relationships between them, it can be understood what kind of data is needed. In this section, we don't consider store internal automation and simply want to mention online store project. There are only two entities in the online store.

1. Customer

2. Products and Services

In software engineering, customer profile, goods and services and type of relationship between them specify data needed to our software. In this section we provide met models of the entities and their relationships. Figure 5-1 illustrates the relationship between the above mentioned entities.

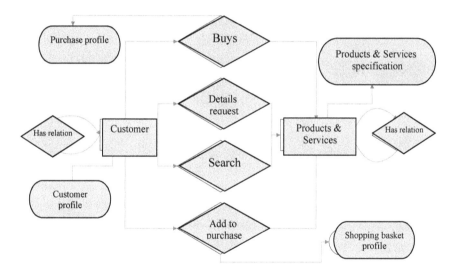

Figure 5-1: Customer Relationship products

1. Customer Profile: As also shown in Figure 4-9, entity of customer profile is stored under the customer's profile. The important point to be considered by web designers is type of goods and profiles that specify type of customers. In other words, by specifying the product, we can also understand the specification of customers' requirements. For example, if the product is a book, it will determine the age and education of customers. Customer profile is composed of two main data groups.

• *Personal information about each customer*: the customer's personal information includes name, surname, age, gender and so on. Different individual customer profiles can be requested for each online store. For instance, if the product of online store is cloth, all bosy sizes is important but if it is a book, there is no need to such specifications.

• *Navigation information about each customer:* in order to have an intelligent website, we must monitor customer behavior on the website and show a proper reaction based on his/her behaviors. Therefore, navigation information of the customer on the website is of a great importance and we need to store them.

2. Goods and services Specifications: these specifications of goods and services are fixed on the website. Only different types of goods and services can have different profiles. For example, if the product is book, he specification we defined for all books must be the same. By changing the type of product, the specification may vary. So its entity is shown in Figure 5-2.

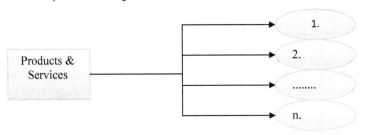

Figure 5-2: entity of goods and services

3. Purchase profiles: purchase is a relationship defined between the product and the customer. Purchase profiles include the information should be recorded in the purchase process. For example, where and when are goods bought by whom? The table should be designed for the relationship can be seen in Figure 5-3.

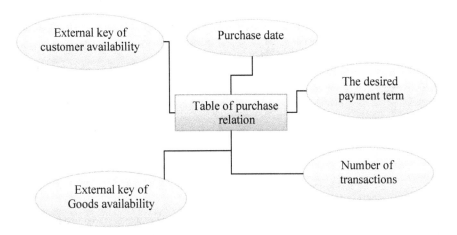

Figure 5-2: Availability of goods and services

4. **Shopping basket profiles**: Shopping basket in e-commerce websites is exactly the same as in the sore. The cart can enable a list of products customer needs to be created. In the list the customer can edit. Edit

means to add or remove products. Finally, when customer decides to buy, the shopping basket will go into the shopping phase. The basket is merely a list of products that the customer has chosen.

5. The other important issue that plays considerable role in intelligent websites is goods relationship and customer relationship with themselves. In modern world Web sites, goods relationship is used in the advertisement. The point is ignored marketers have not in the design of business Web sites, is customers relationship. Customer relationship in a store is obvious. By a little accuracy, you notice that a lot of people who you know purchase from the same stores you purchase. If the e-commerce marketers understand the relationships between customers, they can design a variety of strategies.

6. The above five steps, we talked about needed data. The main point about them is how to store. As said in chapter 4, to implement intelligent websites we need to store data based on RDF. Thus we can model the storage term on a data base by RDF Schema. The mentioned schema specifies type of data relationship in order that we can reach a predicate arising from a raw data and thus it makes RDF meaningful to us. Consequently we have no data but predicate. This subject was discussed in Chapter 2. in this section, for example, we consider a book as a product and type of data modeling is shown in figure1-5.

Object	Predicate	Subject	
C++	Name	Book 1	<Book1, Name, C++>
100	Price	Book 1	<Book1, Author, John>
Ali	Name	Customer 1	<Book1, Price, 100$>
Amir	Name	Customer 2	<Customer1, Name, Ali>
Book 1	Book code	Purchase 1	<Customer1, Age, 25>
Customer 1	Customer code	Purchase 2	<Customer1, Sex, M>
Customer 2	Friend	Customer 1	<Sell1, BookId, Book1>
			< Sell1, CId, Customer1>
			< Sell1, Date, 2 mehr>
			<Customer2, Name, Amir>
			<Customer2, Age, 25>
			<Customer2, Sex, M>
			<Customer1, Friend, C2>

Table 1-5: Instance of RDF predicates and table for how to store

5-2-2 Process Modeling

To model online store process we need to identify the processes. To view processes and their relationships with intra-organizational entities, data flow chart is the best. The data flow diagrams can be viewed in online store.

Figure 5-4: Non-Level Data Flow Diagram

1. Information is entered by Customer:
- Customer gives his/her information.
- Customers requests for information.
- Customer enters purchase information.
- Customers enter search keywords.
- Customer edits information of the shopping basket.

2. Information is received by Customer:
- Customers gets search results.
- Customer view shopping list.
- The Customer receives the requested information.
- Customer will see an error message, if any.
3. Goods Specification is entered.

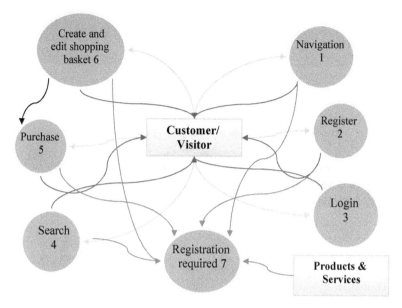

Figure 5-5: Level I Data Flow Diagram

The red vectors represent the necessary information login to the registration process. Orange vectors represent information that customers or clients enter and by the process it is determined what type of information they are entering. Purple vectors return output color or so-called the result of client information processing to them. For more details, you will see the next level data flow diagram.

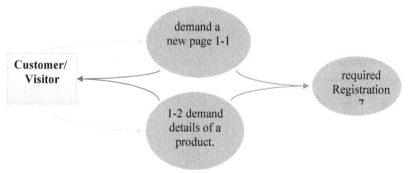

Figure 5-6: Level II Data Flow Diagram - navigation process

As you can see in Figure 5-6, customer navigation is divided into two sub process. When customer click on websites links, or selects an option from existing menus in websites, they all mean a new webpage. In this case, information demand is referred to website by client. Web page shows his/her response. In both cases, goods information is required for the content of the website.

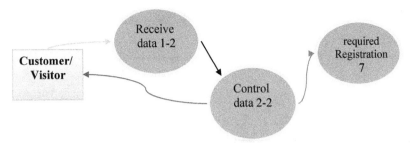

Figure 5-7: Level II Data Flow Diagram -Registration Process

In above figure, at first client enter his/her personal information to register, and then it is controlled to avoid any problem. If there is a problem, a proper message is sent to client and if there is no problem , specific messages are sent and information are prepared to store and finally they are stored in database.

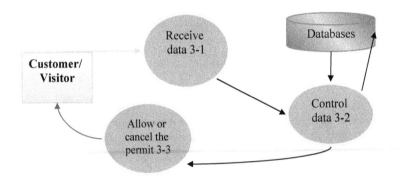

Figure 5-8: Level II Data Flow Diagram -Log Process

As shown in Figure 5-8, information is received from client in process data flow chart. The information contained in the database are compared to be verified their accuracy.

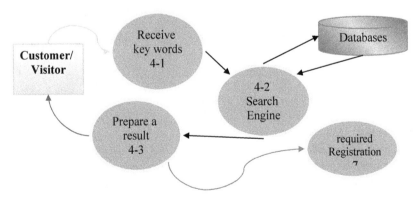

Figure 5-9: Level II Data Flow Diagram -search process

In the search process, as shown in Figure 5-9, client has used the search bar in website and entered the key words. After receiving the search engine keywords, he/she search in a database and the result is announced. Search result is prepared and will be displayed to the user. After preparing the result, words used in this search will be stored in the client profile.

Level II Data Flow Diagram - purchasing process, illustrated in Figure 5-10, is outlined in the purchase process. As cleared in the chart he customer must confirm his/her purchase basket, prepared before, (preparing purchase process will be explained later). After confirmation of the basket, amount payable is calculated and is offered to him/her for a final approval. Issuing final approval, the customer's credit card details by which will be paid is received from him/her. Then a confidential connection to financial institute contain website e-payment is done to complete the process. If the process is done successfully, the customer purchase specifications is stored in his/her purchase list and a proper message is shown to hem/her, otherwise the customer fails to complete the payment . Besides those mentioned, the customer has the ability to see his purchases.

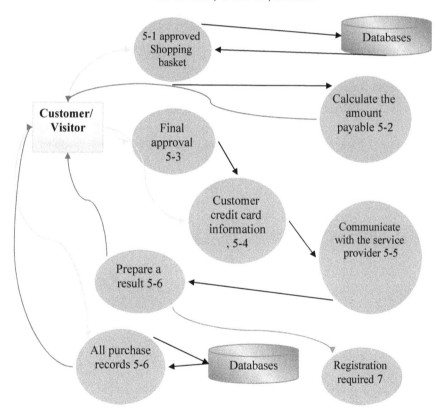

Figure 5-10: Level II Data Flow Diagram - purchasing process

As you can see in Figure 5-11 , the customer must already register for the preparation of shopping basket. Otherwise, he will be transferred temporarily to the registration page. After creating a shopping basket, the customer has ability to add his needed products to it. Add to shopping basket is uncertain, so there is possible to remove. As previously noted, the purchase is finalized when customer approve list of shopping basket to get final approval.

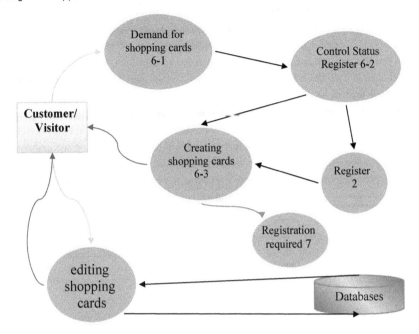

Figure 5-11: Level II Data flow diagram- the process of creating and editing shopping basket

Registration process knows PDF schema. So the information on this standard can be prepared and stored in the database. Data flow diagram is shown in Figure 5-12.

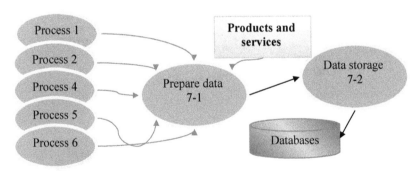

Figure 5-12: Level II Data Flow Diagram - recording process

The above mentioned was all common in all e-commerce Web sites. As you saw in the data flow diagram drawn, for each six available online stores, there was a sub process for preparing the result. The sub processes prepare the content of webpage to visit by client in addition to prepare a result. Intelligent algorithms are implemented by proper sub processes in the websites and client understands the intelligence when to use them. For example, search algorithms applied by search engine or the navigation record navigation algorithms at the time of client control navigation. What is the difference Web sites that are implemented by our proposal design?

The question is considered in modeling process to study mention interact process or in other word, to model the interaction process.

The main difference of our proposed model framework to others is that designers analyzed and implemented their model by object-oriented view. As mentioned in previous chapter, when a client refers to one of modern business websites, all defined processes are available to him/her on the business website. The processes depend on client decision. He/ she uses each one needs or vice versa. As already mentioned, he website operates as information system when the customer does not enter to purchase phase. But the design of our proposed model has no longer object-oriented view it has process-oriented view. This view allows designers to respond to the requested processes. The main difference between object-oriented and process-oriented views can be read in this article. [42]

According to the authors, when designers have process-oriented view, it will create a dialog between the software and user. The dialog that has a hierarchical content structure is customer-oriented. The dialog has one requester that may be client or customer and of respondent. He depicts the mentioned interaction as following figure.

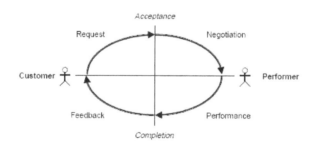

Figure 5-13: Instance of customer- oriented interacts [42]

According to this view, e-commerce Web sites are customers' respondents or web site clients. N our proposed framework, respondent to client is apparently website but is intelligent agent in practice. So this interaction is illustrated in Figure 5-14.

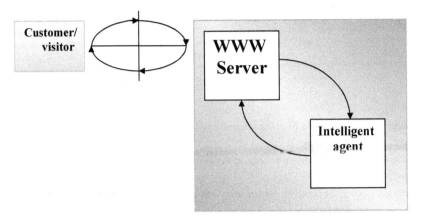

Figure 5-14: How customers interact with web-based business proposal

5-2-3 Users modeling

As noted in the previous sections, goods and services have features by which can specify the type of their users. Every goods has a particular customer. Product specifications determine their customers. Therefore, in User modeling we need to know anything about goods and services. For example, a book determines age and education or even the gender of its reader. Book price can also be a factor to determine the amount of income customer but this is not absolute. So we can reach to user modeling or website clines based on identification the goods and its specifications. The remarkable thing is that user modeling can be done in two stages.

1. The first step: before visiting any customer and recognize the goods and services
2. The Second step, after visiting various clients and collect real information from them.

5-2-4 modeling business

As noted in the 4-2-2-4, modeling, business process modeling business is no difference [40]. There are only a means to implement this package in the middle layer of software that models business process analyst in the previous layer by engineers, is designed. In the modeling business model means the model of a commercial business model. For example, work on modeling sales from eBay auctions on the Web has done.

5-3 final software implementation

5-3-1 Semantic Web standards

The Semantic Web standard is described in section 4-2-3-1.

5-3-2 Semantic Web Applications

The semantic Web applications have been described in section 4-2-3-2.

5-3-3 intelligent interface software

Intelligent software interface was talking about but here are 4-2-3-3 in the form of 5-17 it would kill the image.

As shown in Figure 5-15, the interface software module is 3.

1. The first module is a software module that is responsible for the management of the interaction. This module is the decision maker. The second module is the necessary decisions.

2.The same strategies are strategies for the implementation of the e-commerce marketing, e-commerce Web sites are required. Customer relationship management strategies, for example, that this module knows it.

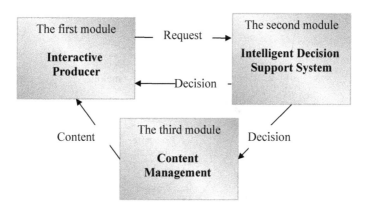

Figure 5-15: Structure of Intelligent agent

3. The third module is a content management module. The first module will deliver the content to the end user to view it.

Is sent to the user... As previously stated, questions based on trade and businesses for different customers, is different.

We assume that users have two categories. To first orders, in the form below to review how they are depicted on the website.

The interaction between the Web client and the image is created Almlhay interaction.

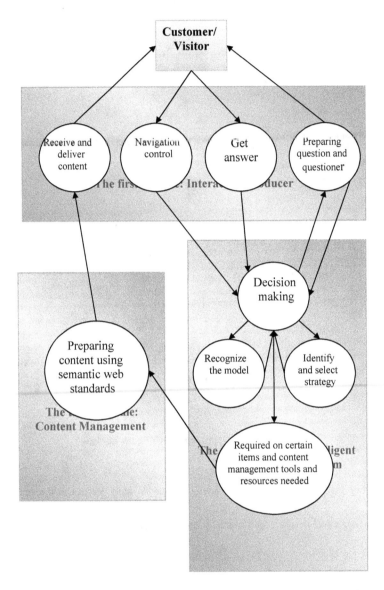

Figure 5-16: Chart of intelligent agent performance

We assume the product is a book for sale on the website.

1. Information that an intelligent software agent should know

A. User Model: As I said before, for a correct model for the receipt of goods for sale to the model. Here is the good book. The book's specifics. Book details are: Name, author, year, author, book publisher's name, age books, science books category, category Science Gender◊ age ◊ education degree ◊ Software ◊ Computer ◊Book

As you can see the profile of a user can specify the type. For example, with age a juvenile cannot be selected by a person of the year. Or a book with the architectural design is chosen by people who do not work in this field. It is noteworthy that there are any goods that may be needed depending on the specification so as to determine its own Karbrsh. For example, if our clothes were good:

Size◊ age ◊ Gender ◊ Culture ◊Clothes

Therefore, a classification for the goods in question, we have a model for the type of Web site users will see we anticipated. Each user can complete model of our potential and to provide a complete profile.
For categorizing the book to be served two ways.
• First method: specify primary keys for the classification of books and special forms when signing Profile Books. Filling out forms and manually enter the specifications, the book is automatically recorded in the categories   will   be   considered.
• The second category of books for specific categories Algvrythmay does data mining. The latest research [50] two algorithms for regression and classification algorithms Nayv Bayes books are the best.
Both models can be classified based on primary keys for the profile to be selected this way: 1. Book 2. Degree   appropriate   to   the   reader   with   three   books.   Genre   book
2. Business model: business, business model and business practices on the Web should know. Or in other words,   policies   and   techniques   for   selling   on   the   web   knows.
3. Marketing, advertising, Web content changes Va Laqa-ye, all of which are customer relationship management.1. When referring to is the new advertising, marketing and Web content according to specification search, it is intended. After the landlord's marketing, advertising and content appropriate to the profile   will   be   created   for   him.
Suppose a user has to first go to our website. On the other hand we also have a website knows that he is a new entrant. We share this website with the key on the computer performs. A person who can go to our website on his computer will be key for future reference and follow-up.
He will be available. This type of effect in the sense of welcome will be referred to a two-way interaction.
Visitors entering the words in your search bar to define its purpose. So try using a search algorithm that aims to convey to the user. Its purpose is to indicate the type of visitor navigation. Our intelligent interface based on the commodity referred to the request, the questions I asked him about getting approved.

The contents are listed as a clearer example.
System is recorded in a book with the following characteristics:
Book: C # programming book Age: 18 years
Author: Deitel & Deitel Category Scientific Books: At least Diploma in Computer
Copyright Year: 2005 field of science: computer
Publication Name: The Nshrlm

A new user will see. And users are welcome to start the C # programming in the search bar. Book smart interface registered in the system with above referred to, and recovery can provide. Immediately referred to a record in the database system is created. As previously mentioned two types of information for each user must be a record. Information 2. Navigation information of the person referred to in the information database is created with a unique code. For example, an interface to the database must be defined.

Last purchase	Last visit date	Course	education	Email	age	surname	Name	Key

Intelligent agent in addition to his estimate, due to the Hdssh web content based on a student's computer to see changes. Perhaps he did not respond to his reaction after the new content will try to get to know him and his administration.

Very optimistic, we assume an intelligent agent referred questions to answer. After attending a student computer. The book details his old age range are defined. So gradually the record is complete for this client. The other identifying characteristics of patients.

Computer	Course	Key of client 1
Computer	Course	Key of client 2
Architecture	Course	Key of client 3
Power- Electronics	Course	Key of client 4
Mathematical	Course	Key of client 5

25	Age	Key of client 1
20	Age	Key of client 2
23	Age	Key of client 3
30	Age	Key of client 4
21	Age	Key of client 5

25	Nationality	Referring to a key
20	Nationality	Referring to two key
23	Nationality	Referred to three key
30	Nationality	Referred to four key
21	Nationality	Referred to five key

Iran	Nationality	Key of client 1
Japan	Nationality	Key of client 2
Canada	Nationality	Key of client 3
Iran	Nationality	Key of client 4
Germany	Nationality	Key of client 5

Ali	Name	Key of client 1
Ehsan	Name	Key of client 2

Amir	Name	Key of client 3
Navid	Name	Key of client 4
Mahmoud	Name	Key of client 5

Navid	Friend	Key of client 1
Amir	Friend	Key of client 2
Ehsan	Friend	Key of client 3
Ali	Friend	Key of client 4

The above mentioned was an example to further clarify the issues. Conclusions and future studies will be studied in the next chapter.

Chapter 6

Conclusion

6-1 Conclusion

As previously noted, due to Internet, there is no space for competitors in business world. Pushing an opponent from the field, only one click is needed. Client attraction and change him/her from a potential to actual is one of important discussion that attracted the view of analysis's, planners and mangers to implement their own new business model, e-commerce. In the thesis, it is hard attempted to identify and resolve missing part in visual e-commerce. This part played a significant role in trade and it has not taken into consideration. Human interacts and feelings that don't exist in e-commerce can be a main factor to lose the customer in every stage of business.

By introducing the proposed plan in the thesis, e-commerce websites can be designed and implemented by the ability to establish a client interaction. The interaction is basis and fundamental of making any human relationships and leads to more identify and establish more relationship. By establishment of intelligent and targeted interaction, the success of business websites in attracting customer is increased and finally by further identification and establishment of intelligent and targeted customer relationship, their confidence and loyalty is increased. The loyalty ensures a long-term success for any business.

6-2 Future studies

The only suggestion for future studies is to implement the proposed framework because capabilities, shortcomings and disadvantages have not been clear yet.